PETER THE GREAT

JACOB ABBOTT

Peter the Great

Jacob Abbott

© 1st World Library, 2007
PO Box 2211
Fairfield, IA 52556
www.1stworldlibrary.com
First Edition

LCCN: 2007934155

Softcover ISBN: 978-1-4218-9652-6
Hardcover ISBN: 978-1-4218-9752-3
eBook ISBN: 978-1-4218-9552-9

Purchase *"Peter the Great"*
as a traditional bound book at:
www.1stWorldLibrary.com/purchase.asp?ISBN=978-1-4218-9652-6

1st World Library is a literary, educational organization
dedicated to:

- Creating a free internet library of downloadable ebooks

- Hosting writing competitions and offering book publishing
scholarships.

Interested in more 1st World Library books? contact:
literacy@1stworldlibrary.com
Check us out at: www.1stworldlibrary.com

1st World Library Literary Society

Giving Back to the World

"If you want to work on the core problem, it's early school literacy."

- James Barksdale, former CEO of Netscape

"No skill is more crucial to the future of a child, or to a democratic and prosperous society, than literacy."

- Los Angeles Times

"Literacy... means far more than learning how to read and write... The aim is to transmit... knowledge and promote social participation."

- UNESCO

"Literacy is not a luxury, it is a right and a responsibility. If our world is to meet the challenges of the twenty-first century we must harness the energy and creativity of all our citizens."

- President Bill Clinton

"Parents should be encouraged to read to their children, and teachers should be equipped with all available techniques for teaching literacy, so the varying needs and capacities of individual kids can be taken into account."

- Hugh Mackay

PREFACE

There are very few persons who have not heard of the fame of Peter the Great, the founder, as he is generally regarded by mankind, of Russian civilization. The celebrity, however, of the great Muscovite sovereign among young persons is due in a great measure to the circumstance of his having repaired personally to Holland, in the course of his efforts to introduce the industrial arts among his people, in order to study himself the art and mystery of shipbuilding, and of his having worked with his own hands in a ship-yard there. The little shop where Peter pursued these practical studies still stands in Saardam, a ship-building town not far from Amsterdam. The building is of wood, and is now much decayed; but, to preserve it from farther injury, it has been incased in a somewhat larger building of brick, and it is visited annually by great numbers of curious travelers.

The whole history of Peter, as might be expected from the indications of character developed by this incident, forms a narrative that is full of interest and instruction for all.

CONTENTS

CHAPTER I

THE PRINCESS SOPHIA

1676-1684

Parentage of Peter—His father's double marriage—Death of his father—The princesses—Their places of seclusion—Theodore and John—Sophia uneasy in the convent—Her request—Her probable motives—Her success—Increase of her influence—Jealousies—Parties formed—The imperial guards—Their character and influence—Dangers—Sophia and the soldiers—Sophia's continued success—Death of Theodore—Peter proclaimed—Plots formed by Sophia—Revolution—Means of exciting the people—Poisoning—Effect of the stories that were circulating—Peter and his mother—The Monastery of the Trinity—Natalia's flight—Narrow escape of Peter—Commotion in the city—Sophia is unsuccessful—Couvansky's schemes—Sophia's attempt to appease the soldiers—No effect produced—Couvansky's views—His plan of a marriage for his son—Indignation of Sophia—A stratagem—Couvansky falls into the snare—Excitement produced by his death—Galitzin—Measures adopted by him—They are successful

The circumstances under which Peter the Great came to the throne form a very remarkable—indeed, in some respects, quite a romantic story.

The name of his father, who reigned as Emperor of Russia from 1645 to 1676, was Alexis Michaelowitz. In the course of his life, this Emperor Alexis was twice married. By his first wife he had two sons, whose names were Theodore and John,[1] and four daughters. The names of the daughters were Sophia, Catharine, Mary, and Sediassa. By his second wife he had two children—a son and a daughter. The name of the son was Peter, and that of the daughter was Natalia Alexowna. Of all these children, those with whom we have most to do are the two oldest sons, Theodore and John, and the oldest daughter, Sophia, by the first wife; and Peter, the oldest son by the second wife, the hero of this history. The name of the second wife, Peter's mother, was Natalia.

Of course, Theodore, at his father's death, was heir to the throne. Next to him in the line of succession came John; and next after John came Peter, the son of the second wife; for, by the ancient laws and usages of the Muscovite monarchy, the daughters were excluded from the succession altogether. Indeed, not only were the daughters excluded themselves from the throne, but special precautions were taken to prevent their ever having sons to lay claim to it. They were forbidden to marry, and, in order to make it impossible that they should ever violate this rule, they were all placed in convents before they arrived at a marriageable age, and were compelled to pass their lives there in seclusion. Of course, the convents where these princesses were lodged were very richly and splendidly endowed, and the royal inmates enjoyed within the walls every comfort and luxury which could possibly be procured for them in such retreats, and which could tend in any measure to reconcile them to being forever debarred from all the pleasures of love and the sweets of domestic life.

Jacob Abbott

Now it so happened that both Theodore and John were feeble and sickly children, while Peter was robust and strong. The law of descent was, however, inexorable, and, on the death of Alexis, Theodore ascended to the throne. Besides, even if it had been possible to choose among the sons of Alexis, Peter was at this time altogether too young to reign, for at his father's death he was only about four years old. He was born in 1672, and his father died in 1676.

Theodore was at this time about sixteen. Of course, however, being so young, and his health being so infirm, he could not take any active part in the administration of government, but was obliged to leave every thing in the hands of his counselors and ministers of state, who managed affairs as they thought proper, though they acted always in Theodore's name.

There were a great many persons who were ambitious of having a share of the power which the young Czar thus left in the hands of his subordinates; and, among these, perhaps the most ambitious of all was the Princess Sophia, Theodore's sister, who was all this time shut up in the convent to which the rules and regulations of imperial etiquette consigned her. She was very uneasy in this confinement, and wished very much to get released, thinking that if she could do so she should be able to make herself of considerable consequence in the management of public affairs. So she made application to the authorities to be allowed to go to the palace to see and take care of her brother in his sickness. This application was at length complied with, and Sophia went to the palace. Here she devoted herself with so much assiduity to the care of her brother, watching constantly at his bedside, and suffering no one to attend upon him or to give him medicines but herself, that she won not only his heart, but the hearts of all the nobles of the court, by her seemingly disinterested sisterly affection.

Indeed, it is not by any means impossible that Sophia might have been at first disinterested and sincere in her desire to minister to the wants of her brother, and to solace and comfort him in his sickness. But, however this may have been at the outset, the result was that, after a time, she acquired so much popularity and influence that she became quite an important personage at court. She was a very talented and accomplished young woman, and was possessed, moreover, of a strong and masculine character. Yet she was very agreeable and insinuating in her manners; and she conversed so affably, and at the same time so intelligently, with all the grandees of the empire, as they came by turns to visit her brother in his sick chamber, that they all formed a very high estimate of her character.

She also obtained a great ascendency over the mind of Theodore himself, and this, of itself, very much increased her importance in the eyes of the courtiers. They all began to think that, if they wished to obtain any favor of the emperor, it was essential that they should stand well with the princess. Thus every one, finding how fast she was rising in influence, wished to have the credit of being her earliest and most devoted friend; so they all vied with each other in efforts to aid in aggrandizing her.

Things went on in this way very prosperously for a time; but at length, as might have been anticipated, suspicions and jealousies began to arise, and, after a time, the elements of a party opposed to the princess began to be developed. These consisted chiefly of the old nobles of the empire, the heads of the great families who had been accustomed, under the emperors, to wield the chief power of the state. These persons were naturally jealous of the ascendency which they saw that the princess was acquiring, and they began to plot together in order to devise means for restricting or controlling it.

Jacob Abbott

But, besides these nobles, there was another very important power at the imperial court at this time, namely, the army. In all despotic governments, it is necessary for the sovereign to have a powerful military force under his command, to maintain him in his place; and it is necessary for him to keep this force as separate and independent as possible from the people. There was in Russia at this time a very powerful body of troops, which had been organized by the emperors, and was maintained by them as an imperial guard. The name of this body of troops was the Strelitz; but, in order not to encumber the narrative unnecessarily with foreign words, I shall call them simply the Guards.

Of course, a body of troops like these, organized and maintained by a despotic dynasty for the express purpose, in a great measure, of defending the sovereign against his subjects, becomes in time a very important element of power in the state. The officers form a class by themselves, separate from, and jealous of the nobles of the country; and this state of things has often led to very serious collisions and outbreaks. The guards have sometimes proved too strong for the dynasty that created them, and have made their own generals the real monarchs of the country. When such a state of things as this exists, the government which results is called a military despotism. This happened in the days of the Roman empire. The army, which was originally formed by the regular authorities of the country, and kept for a time in strict subjection to them, finally became too powerful to be held any longer under control, and they made their own leading general emperor for many successive reigns, thus wholly subverting the republic which originally organized and maintained them.

It was such a military body as this which now possessed great influence and power at Moscow. The Princess Sophia, knowing how important it would be to her to secure the influence of such a power upon her side, paid great attention to the officers, and omitted nothing in her power which was calculated to increase her popularity with the whole corps. The result was that the Guards became her friends, while a great many of the old nobles were suspicious and jealous of her, and were beginning to devise means to curtail her increasing influence.

But, notwithstanding all that they could do, the influence of Sophia increased continually, until the course of public affairs came to be, in fact, almost entirely under her direction. The chief minister of state was a certain Prince Galitzin, who was almost wholly devoted to her interests. Indeed, it was through her influence that he was appointed to his office. Things continued in this state for about six years, and then, at length, Theodore was taken suddenly sick. It soon became evident that he could not live. On his dying bed he designated Peter as his successor, passing over his brother John. The reason for this was that John was so extremely feeble and infirm that he seemed to be wholly unfit to reign over such an empire. Besides various other maladies under which he suffered, he was afflicted with epilepsy, a disease which rendered it wholly unsuitable that he should assume any burdens whatever of responsibility and care.

It is probable that it was through the influence of some of the nobles who were opposed to Sophia that Theodore was induced thus to designate Peter as his successor. However this may be, Peter, though then only ten years old, was proclaimed emperor by the nobles immediately after Theodore's death. Sophia was much disappointed, and became greatly indignant at these proceedings. John was her own brother, while Peter, being a son of the second wife, was only her half-brother. John, too, on account of his feeble health, would probably never be able to take any charge of the government, and she thought that, if he had been allowed to succeed Theodore, she herself might have retained the real power in her hands, as regent, as long as she lived; whereas Peter promised to have strength and vigor to govern the empire himself in a few years, and, in the mean time, while he remained in his minority, it was natural to expect that he would be under the influence of persons connected with his own branch of the family, who would be hostile to her, and that thus her empire would come to an end.

So she determined to resist the transfer of the supreme power to Peter. She secretly engaged the Guards on her side. The commander-in-chief of the Guards was an officer named Couvansky. He readily acceded to her proposals, and, in conjunction with him, she planned and organized a revolution.

In order to exasperate the people and the Guards, and excite them to the proper pitch of violence, Sophia and Couvansky spread a report that the late emperor had not died a natural death, but had been poisoned. This murder had been committed, they said, by a party who hoped, by setting Theodore and his brother John aside, to get the power into their hands in the name of Peter, whom they intended to make emperor, in violation of the rights of John, Theodore's true heir. There was a plan also formed, they said, to poison all the principal officers of the Guards, who, the conspirators knew, would oppose their wicked proceedings, and perhaps prevent the fulfillment of them if they were not put out of the way. The poison by which Theodore had been put to death was administered, they said, by two physicians who attended upon him in his sickness, and who had been bribed to give him poison with his medicine. The Guards were to have been destroyed by means of poison, which was to have been mixed with the brandy and the beer that was distributed to them on the occasion of the funeral.

These stories produced a great excitement among the

Guards, and also among a considerable portion of the people of Moscow. The guards came out into the streets and around the palaces in great force. They first seized the two physicians who were accused of having poisoned the emperor, and killed them on the spot. Then they took a number of nobles of high rank, and officers of state, who were supposed to be the leaders of the party in favor of Peter, and the instigators of the murder of Theodore, and, dragging them out into the public squares, slew them without mercy. Some they cut to pieces. Others they threw down from the wall of the imperial palace upon the soldiers' pikes below, which the men held up for the purpose of receiving them.

Peter was at this time with his mother in the palace. Natalia was exceedingly alarmed, not for herself, but for her son. As soon as the revolution broke out she made her escape from the palace, and set out with Peter in her arms to fly to a celebrated family retreat of the emperor's, called the Monastery of the Trinity. This monastery was a sort of country palace of the Czar's, which, besides being a pleasant rural retreat, was also, from its religious character, a sanctuary where fugitives seeking refuge in it might, under all ordinary circumstances, feel themselves beyond the reach of violence and of every species of hostile molestation.

Natalia fled with Peter and a few attendants to this refuge, hotly pursued, however, all the way by a body of the Guards. If the fugitives had been overtaken on the way, both mother and son would doubtless have been cut to pieces without mercy. As it was, they very narrowly escaped, for when Natalia arrived at the convent the soldiers were close upon her. Two of them followed her in before the doors could be closed. Natalia rushed into the church, which formed the centre of the convent inclosure, and took refuge with her child at the foot of the altar. The soldiers pursued her there, brandishing their swords, and were apparently on the point

Jacob Abbott

of striking the fatal blow; but the sacredness of the place seemed to arrest them at the last moment, and, after pausing an instant with their uplifted swords in their hands, and uttering imprecations against their victims for having thus escaped them, they sullenly retired.

In the mean time the commotion in the city went on, and for several days no one could foresee how it would end. At length a sort of compromise was effected, and it was agreed by the two parties that John should be proclaimed Czar, not alone, but in conjunction with his brother Peter, the regency to remain for the present, as it had been, in the hands of Sophia. Thus Sophia really gained all her ends; for the retaining of Peter's name, as nominally Czar in conjunction with his brother, was of no consequence, since her party had proved itself the strongest in the struggle, and all the real power remained in her hands. She had obtained this triumph mainly through Couvansky and the Guards; and now, having accomplished her purposes by means of their military violence, she wished, of course, that they should retire to their quarters, and resume their habits of subordination, and of submission to the civil authority. But this they would not do. Couvansky, having found how important a personage he might become through the agency of the terrible organization which was under his direction and control, was not disposed at once to lay aside his power; and the soldiers, intoxicated with the delights of riot and pillage, could not now be easily restrained. Sophia found, as a great many other despotic rulers have done in similar cases, that she had evoked a power which she could not now control. Couvansky and the troops under his command continued their ravages in the city, plundering the rich houses of every thing that could gratify their appetites and passions, and murdering all whom they imagined to belong to the party opposed to them.

Sophia first tried to appease them and reduce them to order

by conciliatory measures. From the Monastery of the Trinity, to which she had herself now retreated for safety, she sent a message to Couvansky and to the other chiefs of the army, thanking them for the zeal which they had shown in revenging the death of her brother, the late emperor, and in vindicating the rights of the true successor, John, and promising to remember, and in due time to reward, the great services which they had rendered to the state. She added that, now, since the end which they all had in view in the movement which they had made had been entirely and happily accomplished, the soldiers should be restrained from any farther violence, and recalled to their quarters.

This message had no effect. Indeed, Couvansky, finding how great the power was of the corps which he commanded, began to conceive the idea that he might raise himself to the supreme command. He thought that the Guards were all devoted to him, and would do whatever he required of them. He held secret conferences with the principal officers under his command, and endeavored to prepare their minds for the revolution which he contemplated by representing to them that neither of the princes who had been proclaimed were fit to reign. John, he said, was almost an imbecile, on account of the numerous and hopeless bodily infirmities to which he was subject. Peter was yet a mere boy; and then, besides, even when he should become a man, he would very likely be subject to the same diseases with his brother. These men would never have either the intelligence to appreciate or the power to reward such services as the Guards were capable of rendering to the state; whereas he, their commander, and one of their own body, would be both able and disposed to do them ample justice.

Couvansky also conceived the design of securing and perpetuating the power which he hoped thus to acquire through the army by a marriage of his son with one of the

Jacob Abbott

princesses of the imperial family. He selected Catharine, who was Sophia's sister—the one next in age to her—for the intended bride. He cautiously proposed this plan to Sophia, hoping that she might be induced to approve and favor it, in which case he thought that every obstacle would be removed from his way, and the ends of his ambition would be easily and permanently attained.

But Sophia was perfectly indignant at such a proposal. It seemed to her the height of presumption and audacity for a mere general in the army to aspire to a connection by marriage with the imperial family, and to a transfer, in consequence, of the supreme power to himself and to his descendants forever. She resolved immediately to adopt vigorous measures to defeat these schemes in the most effectual manner. She determined to kill Couvansky. But, as the force which he commanded was so great that she could not hope to accomplish any thing by an open contest, she concluded to resort to stratagem. She accordingly pretended to favor Couvansky's plans, and seemed to be revolving in her mind the means of carrying them into effect. Among other things, she soon announced a grand celebration of the Princess Catharine's fete-day, to be held at the Monastery of the Trinity, and invited Couvansky to attend it.[2] Couvansky joyfully accepted this invitation, supposing that the occasion would afford him an admirable opportunity to advance his views in respect to his son. So Couvansky, accompanied by his son, set out on the appointed day from Moscow to proceed to the monastery. Not suspecting any treachery, he was accompanied by only a small escort. On the road he was waylaid by a body of two hundred horsemen, whom Galitzin, Sophia's minister of state, had sent to the spot. Couvansky's guard was at once over-powered, and both he and his son were taken prisoners. They were hurried at once to a house, where preparations for receiving them had already been made, and there, without any delay, sentence of death against them both, on a charge of treason, was read to them, and their heads were cut off on the spot.

The news of this execution spread with great rapidity, and it produced, of course, an intense excitement and commotion among all the Guards as fast as it became known to them. They threatened vengeance against the government for having thus assassinated, as they expressed it, their chief and father. They soon put themselves in motion, and began murdering, plundering, and destroying more furiously than ever. The violence which they displayed led to a reaction. A party was formed, even among the Guards, of persons that were disposed to discountenance these excesses, and even to submit to the government. The minister Galitzin took advantage of these dissensions to open a communication with those who were disposed to return to their duty. He managed the affair so well that, in the end, the great body of the soldiers were brought over, and, finally, they themselves, of their own accord, slew the officers who had been most active in the revolt, and offered their heads to the minister in token of their submission. They also implored pardon of the government for the violence and excess into which they had been led. Of course, this pardon was readily granted. The places of Couvansky and of the other officers who had been slain were filled by new appointments, who were in the interest of the Princess Sophia, and the whole corps returned to their duty. Order was now soon fully restored in Moscow, rendering it safe for Sophia and her court to leave the monastery and return to the royal palace in the town. Galitzin was promoted to a higher office, and invested with more extended powers than he had yet held, and Sophia found herself finally established as the real sovereign of the country, though, of course, she reigned, in the name of her brothers.

[1] The Russian form of these names is Foedor [Transcriber's

Jacob Abbott

note: Feodor?] and Ivan.

[2] These celebrations were somewhat similar to the birthday celebrations of England and America, only the day on which they were held was not the birth-day of the lady, but the fete-day, as it was called, of her patron saint—that is, of the saint whose name she bore. All the names for girls used in those countries where the Greek or the Catholic Church prevails are names of saints, each one of whom has in the calendar a certain day set apart as her fete-day. Each girl considers the saint from whom she is named as her patron saint, and the fete-day of this saint, instead of her own birth-day, is the anniversary which is celebrated in honor of her.

CHAPTER II

THE PRINCESS'S DOWNFALL

1684-1869

Sophia at the height of her power—Military expeditions—The Cham of Tartary—Mazeppa—Origin and history—His famous punishment—Subsequent history—The war unsuccessful—Sophia's artful policy—Rewards and honors to the army—The opposition—Their plans—Reasons for the proposed marriage—The intended wife—Motives of politicians—Results of Peter's marriage—Peter's country house—Return of Galitzin—The princess's alarm—The Cossacks—Sophia's plot—The commander of the Guards—Prince Galitzin—Details of the plot—Manner in which the plot was discovered—Messengers dispatched—The sentinels—The detachment arrives—Peter's place of refuge—Sophia's pretenses—The Guards—Sophia attempts to secure them—They adhere to the cause of Peter—Sophia's alarm—Her first deputation—Failure of the deputation—Sophia appeals to the patriarch—His mission fails—Sophia's despair—Her final plans—She is repulsed from the monastery—The surrender of Thekelavitaw demanded—He is brought to trial—He is put to the torture—His confessions—Value of them—Modes of torture applied—Various punishments inflicted—Galitzin is banished—His son shares his fate—Punishment of Thekelavitaw—Decision in respect to Sophia—Peter's public entry into Moscow—He gains sole power—Character and condition of John—Subsequent history of Sophia

The Princess Sophia was now in full possession of power, so that she reigned supreme in the palaces and in the capital, while, of course, the ordinary administration of the affairs of state, and the relations of the empire with foreign nations, were left to Galitzin and the other ministers. It was in 1684 that she secured possession of this power, and in 1689 her regency came to an end, so that she was, in fact, the ruler of the Russian empire for a period of about five years.

During this time one or two important military expeditions were set on foot by her government. The principal was a campaign in the southern part of the empire for the conquest of the Crimea, which country, previous to that time, had belonged to the Turks. Poland was at that period a very powerful kingdom, and the Poles, having become involved in a war with the Turks, proposed to the Russians, or Muscovites, as they were then generally called, to join them in an attempt to conquer the Crimea. The Tartars who inhabited the Crimea and the country to the northeastward of it were on the side of the Turks, so that the Russians had two enemies to contend with.

The supreme ruler of the Tartars was a chieftain called a Cham. He was a potentate of great power and dignity, superior, indeed, to the Czars who ruled in Muscovy. In fact, there had been an ancient treaty by which this superiority of the Cham was recognized and acknowledged in a singular way—one which illustrates curiously the ideas and manners of those times. The treaty stipulated, among other things, that whenever the Czar and the Cham should chance to meet, the Czar should hold the Cham's stirrup while he mounted his horse, and also feed the horse with oats out of his cap.

In the war between the Muscovites and the Tartars for the possession of the Crimea, a certain personage appeared, who has since been made very famous by the poetry of Byron. It was Mazeppa, the unfortunate chieftain whose frightful ride through the tangled thickets of an uncultivated country, bound naked to a wild horse, was described with so much graphic power by the poet, and has been so often represented in paintings and engravings.

Mazeppa was a Polish gentleman. He was brought up as a page in the family of the King of Poland. When he became a man he mortally offended a certain Polish nobleman by some improprieties in which he became involved with the nobleman's wife. The husband caused him to be seized and cruelly scourged, and then to be bound upon the back of a wild, ungovernable horse. When all was ready the horse was turned loose upon the Ukrain, and, terrified with the extraordinary burden which he felt upon his back, and uncontrolled by bit or rein, he rushed madly on through the wildest recesses of the forest, until at length he fell down exhausted with terror and fatigue. Some Cossack peasants found and rescued Mazeppa, and took care of him in one of their huts until he recovered from his wounds.

Mazeppa was a well-educated man, and highly accomplished in the arts of war as they were practiced in those days. He soon acquired great popularity among the Cossacks, and, in the end, rose to be a chieftain among them, and he distinguished himself greatly in these very campaigns in the Crimea, fought by the Muscovites against the Turks and Tartars during the regency of the Princess Sophia.

If the war thus waged by the government of the empress had been successful, it would have greatly strengthened the

Jacob Abbott

position of her party in Moscow, and increased her own power; but it was not successful. Prince Galitzin, who had the chief command of the expedition, was obliged, after all, to withdraw his troops from the country, and make a very unsatisfactory peace; but he did not dare to allow the true result of the expedition to be known in Moscow, for fear of the dissatisfaction which, he felt convinced, would be occasioned there by such intelligence; and the distance was so great, and the means of communication in those days were so few, that it was comparatively easy to falsify the accounts. So, after he had made peace with the Tartars, and began to draw off his army, he sent couriers to Moscow to the Czars, and also to the King in Poland, with news of great victories which he had obtained against the Tartars, of conquests which he made in their territories, and of his finally having compelled them to make peace on terms extremely favorable. The Princess Sophia, as soon as this news reached her in Moscow, ordered that arrangements should be made for great public rejoicings throughout the empire on account of the victories which had been obtained. According to the custom, too, of the Muscovite government, in cases where great victories had been won, the council drew up a formal letter of thanks and commendations to the officers and soldiers of the army, and sent it to them by a special messenger, with promotions and other honors for the chiefs, and rewards in money for the men. The princess and her government hoped, by these means, to conceal the bad success of their enterprise, and to gain, instead of losing, credit and strength with the people.

But during all this time a party opposed to Sophia and her plans had been gradually forming, and it was now increasing in numbers and influence every day. The men of this party naturally gathered around Peter, intending to make him their leader. Peter had now grown up to be a young man. In the next chapter we shall give some account of the manner in which his childhood and early youth were spent; but he was now about eighteen years old, and the party who adhered to him formed the plan of marrying him. So they proceeded to choose him a wife.

The reasons which led them to advocate this measure were, of course, altogether political. They thought that if Peter were to be married, and to have children, all the world would see that the crown must necessarily descend in his family, since John had no children, and he was so sickly and feeble that it was not probable that even he himself would long survive. They knew very well, therefore, that the marriage of Peter and the birth of an heir would turn all men's thoughts to him as the real personage whose favor it behooved them to cultivate; and this, they supposed, would greatly increase his importance, and so add to the strength of the party that acted in his name.

It turned out just as they had anticipated. The wife whom the councilors chose for Peter was a young lady of noble birth, the daughter of one of the great boiars, as they were called, of the empire. Her name was Ottokessa Federowna. The Princess Sophia did all in her power to prevent the match, but her efforts were of no avail. Peter was married, and the event greatly increased his importance among the nobles and among the people, and augmented the power and influence of his party. In all cases of this kind, where a contest is going on between rival claimants to a throne, or rival dynasties, there are some persons, though not many, who are governed in their conduct, in respect to the side which they take, by principles of honor and duty, and of faithful adherence to what they suppose to be the right. But a vast majority of courtiers and politicians in all countries and in all ages are only anxious to find out, not which side is right, but which is likely to be successful. Accordingly, in this case, as the marriage of Peter made it still more probable than it was before that he would in the end secure to his branch of the family the supreme power, it greatly increased the tendency among the nobles to pay their court to him and to his friends. This tendency was still more strengthened by the expectation which soon after arose, that Peter's wife was about to give birth to a son. The probability of the appearance of a son and heir on Peter's side, taken in connection with the hopeless childlessness of John, seemed to turn the scales entirely in favor of Peter's party. This was especially the case in respect to all the young nobles as they successively arrived at an age to take an interest in public affairs. All these young men seemed to despise the imbecility, and the dark and uncertain prospects of John, and to be greatly charmed with the talents and energy of Peter, and with the brilliant future which seemed to be opening before him. Thus even the nobles who still adhered to the cause of Sophia and of John had the mortification to find that their sons, as fast as they came of age, all went over to the other side.

Peter lived at this time with his young wife at a certain country palace belonging to him, situated on the banks of a small river a few miles from Moscow. The name of this country-seat was Obrogensko.

Such was the state of things at Moscow when Prince Galitzin returned from his campaigns in the Crimea. The prince found that the power of Sophia and her party was rapidly waning, and that Sophia herself was in a state of great anxiety and excitement in respect to the future. The princess gave Galitzin a very splendid reception, and publicly rewarded him for his pretended success in the war by bestowing upon him great and extraordinary honors. Still many people were very suspicious of the truth of the accounts which were circulated. The partisans of Peter called for proofs that the victories had really been won. Prince Galitzin brought with him to the capital a considerable force of Cossacks, with

Mazeppa at their head. The Cossacks had never before been allowed to come into Moscow; but now, Sophia having formed a desperate plan to save herself from the dangers that surrounded her, and knowing that these men would unscrupulously execute any commands that were given to them by their leaders, directed Galitzin to bring them within the walls, under pretense to do honor to Mazeppa for the important services which he had rendered during the war. But this measure was very unpopular with the people, and, although the Cossacks were actually brought within the walls, they were subjected to such restrictions there that, after all, Sophia could not employ them for the purpose of executing her plot, but was obliged to rely on the regular Muscovite troops of the imperial Guard.

The plot which she formed was nothing else than the assassination of Peter. She saw no other way by which she could save herself from the dangers which surrounded her, and make sure of retaining her power. Her brother, the Czar John, was growing weaker and more insignificant every day; while Peter and his party, who looked upon her, she knew, with very unfriendly feelings, were growing stronger and stronger. If Peter continued to live, her speedy downfall, she was convinced, was sure. She accordingly determined that Peter should die.

The commander-in-chief of the Guards at this time was a man named Theodore Thekelavitaw. He had been raised to this exalted post by Sophia herself on the death of Couvansky. She had selected him for this office with special reference to his subserviency to her interests. She determined now, accordingly, to confide to him the execution of her scheme for the assassination of Peter.

When Sophia proposed her plan to Prince Galitzin, he was at first strongly opposed to it, on account of the desperate danger which would attend such an undertaking. But she urged upon him so earnestly the necessity of the case, representing to him that unless some very decisive measures were adopted, not only would she herself soon be deposed from power, but that he and all his family and friends would be involved in the same common ruin, he at length reluctantly consented.

The plan was at last fully matured. Thekelavitaw, the commander of the Guards, selected six hundred men to go with him to Obrogensko. They were to go in the night, the plan being to seize Peter in his bed. When the appointed night arrived, the commander marshaled his men and gave them their instructions, and the whole body set out upon their march to Obrogensko with every prospect of successfully accomplishing the undertaking.

But the whole plan was defeated in a very remarkable manner. While the commander was giving his instructions to the men, two of the soldiers, shocked with the idea of being made the instruments of such a crime, stole away unobserved in the darkness, and ran with all possible speed to Obrogensko to warn Peter of his danger. Peter leaped from his bed in consternation, and immediately sent to the apartments where his uncles, the brothers of his mother, were lodging, to summon them to come to him. When they came, a hurried consultation was held. There was some doubt in the minds of Peter's uncles whether the story which the soldiers told was to be believed. They thought it could not possibly be true that so atrocious a crime could be contemplated by Sophia. Accordingly, before taking any measures for sending Peter and his family away, they determined to send messengers toward the city to ascertain whether any detachment of Guards was really coming toward Obrogensko.

These messengers set off at once; but, before they had

reached half way to Moscow, they met Thekelavitaw's detachment of Guards, with Thekelavitaw himself at the head of them, stealing furtively along the road. The messengers hid themselves by the wayside until the troop had gone by. Then hurrying away round by a circuitous path, they got before the troop again, and reached the palace before the assassins arrived. Peter had just time to get into a coach, with his wife, his sister, and one or two other members of his family, and to drive away from the palace before Thekelavitaw, with his band, arrived. The sentinels who were on duty at the gates of the palace had been much surprised at the sudden departure of Peter and his family, and now they were astonished beyond measure at the sudden appearance of so large a body of their comrades arriving at midnight, without any warning, from the barracks in Moscow.

Immediately on his arrival at the palace, Thekelavitaw's men searched every where for Peter, but of course could not find him. They then questioned the sentinels, and were told that Peter had left the palace with his family in a very hurried manner but a very short time before. No one knew where they had gone.

There was, of course, nothing now for Thekelavitaw to do but to return, discomfited and alarmed, to the Princess Sophia, and report the failure of their scheme.

In the mean time Peter had fled to the Monastery of the Trinity, the common refuge of the family in all cases of desperate danger. The news of the affair spread rapidly, and produced universal excitement. Peter, from his retreat in the monastery, sent a message to Sophia, charging her with having sent Thekelavitaw and his band to take his life. Sophia was greatly alarmed at the turn which things had taken. She, however, strenuously denied being guilty of the

Jacob Abbott

charge which Peter made against her. She said that the soldiers under Thekelavitaw had only gone out to Obrogensko for the purpose of relieving the guard. This nobody believed. The idea of taking such a body of men a league or more into the country at midnight for the purpose of relieving the guard of a country palace was preposterous.

The excitement increased. The leading nobles of the country began to flock to the monastery to declare their adhesion to Peter, and their determination to sustain and protect him. Sophia, at the same time, did all that she could do to rally her friends. Both sides endeavored to gain the good-will of the Guards. The princess caused them to be assembled before her palace in Moscow, and there she appeared on a balcony before them, accompanied by the Czar John; and the Czar made them a speech—one, doubtless, which Sophia had prepared for him. In this speech John stated to the Guards that his brother Peter had retired to the Monastery of the Trinity, though for what reason he knew not. He had, however, too much reason to fear, he said, that he was plotting some schemes against the state.

"We have heard," he added, "that he has summoned you to repair thither and attend him, but we forbid your going on pain of death."

Sophia then herself addressed the Guards, confirming what John had said, and endeavoring artfully to awaken an interest in their minds in her favor. The Guards listened in silence; but it seems that very little effect was produced upon them by these harangues, for they immediately afterward marched in a body to the monastery, and there publicly assured Peter of their adhesion to his cause.

Sophia was now greatly alarmed. She began to fear that all was lost. She determined to send an embassage to Peter to deprecate his displeasure, and, if possible, effect a reconciliation. She employed on this commission two of her aunts, her father's sisters, who were, of course, the aunts likewise of Peter, and the nearest family relatives, who were equally the relatives of herself and of him. These ladies were, of course, princesses of very high rank, and their age and family connection were such as to lead Sophia to trust a great deal to their intercession.

She charged these ladies to assure Peter that she was entirely innocent of the crime of which she was suspected, and that the stories of her having sent the soldiers to his palace with any evil design were fabricated by her enemies, who wished to sow dissension between herself and him. She assured him that there had been no necessity at all for his flight, and that he might now at any time return to Moscow with perfect safety.

Peter received his aunts in a very respectful manner, and listened attentively to what they had to say; but, after they had concluded their address to him, he assured them that his retreat to the monastery was not without good cause: and he proceeded to state and explain all the circumstances of the case, and to show so many and such conclusive proofs that a conspiracy to destroy him had actually been formed, and was on the eve of being executed, that the princesses could no longer doubt that Sophia was really guilty. They were overwhelmed with grief in coming to this conviction, and they declared, with tears in their eyes, that they would not return to Moscow, but would remain at the monastery and share the fortunes of their nephew.

When Sophia learned what had been the result of her deputation she was more alarmed than ever. After spending some time in perplexity and distress, she determined to apply to the patriarch, who was the head of the Church, and, of course, the highest ecclesiastical dignitary in the empire. She begged and implored him to act as mediator between her and her brother, and he was at length so moved by her tears and entreaties that he consented to go.

This embassage was no more successful than the other. Peter, it seems, was provided with proof, which he offered to the patriarch, not only of the reality of the conspiracy which had been formed, but also of the fact that, if it had been successful, the patriarch himself was to have been taken off, in order that another ecclesiastic more devoted to Sophia's interests might be put in his place. The patriarch was astonished and shocked at this intelligence, and was so much alarmed by it that he did not dare to return to Sophia to make his report, and decided, as the ladies had done before him, to take up his abode with Peter in the monastery until the crisis should be passed.

The princess was now almost in a state of despair. Prince Galitzin, it is true, still remained with her, and there were some others in the palace who adhered to her cause. She called these few remaining friends together, and with them held a sorrowful and anxious consultation, in order to determine what should now be done. It was resolved that Thekelavitaw and one or two others who were deeply implicated in the plot for the assassination of Peter should be secured in a place of close concealment in the palace, and then, that the princess herself, accompanied by Galitzin and her other leading friends, should proceed in a body to the Monastery of the Trinity, and there make a personal appeal to Peter, in hopes of appeasing him, and saving themselves, if possible, from their impending fate. This plan they proceeded to carry into effect; but before Sophia, and those who were with her, had reached half way to the palace, they were met by a nobleman who had been sent from the monastery to intercept them, and order them, in Peter's name, to return to Moscow. If the princess were to go on, she would not be received at the monastery, the messenger said, but would find the gates closed against her.

So Sophia and her train turned, and despairingly retraced their steps to Moscow.

The next day an officer, at the head of a body of the Guards three hundred in number, was dispatched from the monastery to demand of the Princess Sophia, at her palace, that she should give up Thekelavitaw, in order that he might be brought to trial on a charge of treason. Sophia was extremely unwilling to comply with this demand. She may naturally be supposed to have desired to save her instrument and agent from suffering the penalties of the crime which she herself had planned and had instigated him to attempt; but the chief source of her extreme reluctance to surrender the prisoner was her fear of the revelations which he would be likely to make implicating her. After hesitating for a time, being in a state during the interval of great mental distress and anguish, she concluded that she must obey, and so Thekelavitaw was brought out from his retreat and surrendered. The soldiers immediately took him and some other persons who were surrendered with him, and, securing them safely with irons, they conveyed them rapidly to the monastery.

Thekelavitaw was brought to trial in the great hall of the monastery, where a court, consisting of the leading nobles, was organized to hear his cause. He was questioned closely by his judges for a long time, but his answers were evasive and unsatisfactory, and at length it was determined to put him to torture, in order to compel him to confess his crime, and to reveal the names of his confederates. This was a very unjust and cruel mode of procedure, but it was in accordance with the rude ideas which prevailed in those times.

Jacob Abbott

The torture which was applied to Thekelavitaw was scourging with a knout. The knout was a large and strong whip, the lash of which consists of a tough, thick thong of leather, prepared in a particular way, so as greatly to increase the intensity of the agony caused by the blows inflicted with it. Thekelavitaw endured a few strokes from this dreadful instrument, and then declared that he was ready to confess all; so they took him back to prison and there heard what he had to say. He made a full statement in respect to the plot. He said that the design was to kill Peter himself, his mother, and several other persons, near connections of Peter's branch of the family. The Princess Sophia was the originator of the plot, he said, and he specified many other persons who had taken a leading part in it.

These statements of the unhappy sufferer may have been true or they may have been false. It is now well known that no reliance whatever can be placed upon testimony that is extorted in this way, as men under such circumstances will say any thing which they think will be received by their tormentors, and be the means of bringing their sufferings to an end.

However it may have been in fact in this case, the testimony of Thekelavitaw was believed. On the faith of it many more arrests were made, and many other persons were put to the torture to compel them to reveal additional particulars of the plot. It is said that one of the modes of torment of the sufferers in these trials consisted in first shaving the head and tying it in a fixed position, and then causing boiling water to be poured, drop by drop, upon it, which in a very short time produced, it is said, an exquisite and dreadful agony which no mortal heroism could long endure.

After all these extorted confessions had been received, and the persons accused by the wretched witnesses had been secured, the court was employed two days in determining the relative guilt of the different criminals, and in deciding upon the punishments. Some of the prisoners were beheaded; others were sentenced to perpetual imprisonment; others were banished. The punishment of Prince Galitzin was banishment for life to Siberia. He was brought before the court to hear his sentence pronounced by the judges in form. It was to this effect, namely, "That he was ordered to go to Karga, a town under the pole, there to remain, as long as he lived, in disgrace with his majesty, who had, nevertheless, of his great goodness, allowed him threepence a day for his subsistence; but that his justice had ordained all his goods to be forfeited to his treasury."

Galitzin had a son who seems to have been implicated in some way with his father in the conspiracy. At any rate, he was sentenced to share his father's fate. Whether the companionship of his son on the long and gloomy journey was a comfort to the prince, or whether it only redoubled the bitterness of his calamity to see his son compelled to endure it too, it would be difficult to say. The female members of the family were sent with them too.

As soon as the prince had been sent away, officers were dispatched to take possession of his palace, and to make an inventory of the property contained in it. The officers found a vast amount of treasure. Among other things, they discovered a strong box buried in a vault, which contained an immense sum of money. There were four hundred vessels of silver of great weight, and many other rich and costly articles. All these things were confiscated, and the proceeds put into the imperial treasury.

Thekelavitaw, the commander-in-chief of the Guards, had his head cut off. The subordinate officer who had the immediate command of the detachment which marched out

Jacob Abbott

to Obrogensko was punished by being first scourged with the knout, then having his tongue cut out, and then being sent to Siberia in perpetual banishment, with an allowance for his subsistence of one third the pittance which had been granted to Galitzin. Some of the private soldiers of the detachment were also sentenced to have their tongues cut out, and then to be sent to Siberia to earn their living there by hunting sables.

Peter was not willing that the Princess Sophia, being his sister, should be publicly punished or openly disgraced in any way, so it was decreed that she should retire to a certain convent, situated in a solitary place a little way out of town, where she could be closely watched and guarded. Sophia was extremely unwilling to obey this decree, and she would not go to the convent of her own accord. The commander of the Guards was thereupon directed to send a body of armed men to convey her there, with orders to take her by force if she would not go willingly; so Sophia was compelled to submit, and, when she was lodged in the convent, soldiers were placed not only to keep sentinel at the doors, but also to guard all the avenues leading to the place, so as effectually to cut the poor prisoner off from all possible communication with any who might be disposed to sympathize with her or aid her. She remained in this condition, a close prisoner, for many years.

Two days after this—every thing connected with the conspiracy having been settled—it was determined that Peter should return to Moscow. He made a grand triumphant entry into the city, attended by an armed escort of eighteen thousand of the Guards. Peter himself rode conspicuously at the head of the troops on horseback. His wife and his mother followed in a coach.

On arriving at the royal palace, he was met on the staircase by his brother John, who was not supposed to have taken any part in Sophia's conspiracy. Peter greeted his brother kindly, and said he hoped that they were friends. John replied in the same spirit, and so the two brothers were reinstated again as joint possessors, nominally, of the supreme power, but, now that Sophia was removed out of the way, and all her leading friends and partisans were either beheaded or banished, the whole control of the government fell, in fact, into the hands of Peter and of his counselors and friends.

John, his brother Czar, was too feeble and inefficient to take any part whatever in the management of public affairs. He was melancholy and dejected in spirit, in consequence of his infirmities and sufferings, and he spent most of his time in acts of devotion, according to the rites and usages of the established church of the country, as the best means within his knowledge of preparing himself for another and happier world. He died about seven years after this time.

The Princess Sophia lived for fifteen years a prisoner. During this period several efforts were made by those who still adhered to her cause to effect her release and her restoration to power, but they were all unsuccessful. She remained in close confinement as long as she lived.

Jacob Abbott

CHAPTER III

THE CHILDHOOD AND YOUTH OF PETER

1677-1688

Troublous times in the family—Peter's first governor—His qualifications—Peter's earliest studies—His disposition and character—Sophia's jealousy of him—Her plans for corrupting his morals—The governor is dismissed—New system adopted—Sophia's expectations—Peter's fifty playmates—The plot does not succeed—Peter organizes a military school—Peter a practical mechanic—His ideas and intentions—His drumming—His wheelbarrow—Progress of the school—Results of Peter's energy of character

We must now go back a little in our narrative, in order to give some account of the manner in which the childhood and early youth of Peter were spent, and of the indications which appeared in this early period of his life to mark his character. He was only eighteen years of age at the time of his marriage, and, of course, all those contests and dissensions which, for so many years after his father Alexis's death, continued to distract the family, took place while he was very young. He was only about nine years old when they began, at the time of the death of his father.

The person whom Peter's father selected to take charge of his little son's education, in the first instance, was a very accomplished general named Menesius. General Menesius was a Scotchman by birth, and he had been well educated in the literary seminaries of his native country, so that, besides his knowledge and skill in every thing which pertained to the art of war, he was well versed in all the European languages, and, having traveled extensively in the different countries of Europe, he was qualified to instruct Peter, when he should become old enough to take an interest in such inquiries, in the arts and sciences of western Europe, and in the character of the civilization of the various countries, and the different degrees of progress which they had respectively made.

At the time, however, when Peter was put under his governor's charge he was only about five years old, and, consequently, none but the most elementary studies were at that time suited to his years. Of course, it was not the duty of General Menesius to attend personally to the instruction of his little pupil in these things, but only to see to it that the proper teachers were appointed, and that they attended to their duties in a faithful manner.

Every thing went on prosperously and well under this arrangement as long as the Czar Alexis, Peter's father, continued to live. General Menesius resided in the palace with his charge, and he gradually began to form a strong attachment to him. Indeed, Peter was so full of life and spirit, and evinced so much intelligence in all that he did and said, and learned what was proper to be taught him at that age with so much readiness and facility, that he was a favorite with all who knew him; that is, with all who belonged to or were connected with his mother's branch of the family. With those who were connected with the children of Alexis' first wife he was an object of continual jealousy and suspicion, and the greater the proofs that he gave of talent and capacity, the more jealous of him these his natural rivals became.

At length, when Alexis, his father, died, and his half-brother Theodore succeeded to the throne, the division between the two branches of the family became more decided than ever; and when Sophia obtained her release from the convent, and managed to get the control of public affairs, in consequence of Theodore's imbecility, as related in the first chapter, one of the first sources of uneasiness for her, in respect to the continuance of her power, was the probability that Peter would grow up to be a talented and energetic young man, and would sooner or later take the government into his own hands. She revolved in her mind many plans for preventing this. The one which seemed to her most feasible at first was to attempt to spoil the boy by indulgence and luxury.

She accordingly, it is said, attempted to induce Menesius to alter the arrangements which he had made for Peter, so as to release him from restraint, and allow him to do as he pleased. Her plan was also to supply him with means of pleasure and indulgence very freely, thinking that a boy of his age would not have the good sense or the resolution to resist these temptations. Thus she thought that his progress in study would be effectually impeded, and that, perhaps, he would undermine his health and destroy his constitution by eating and drinking, or by other hurtful indulgences.

But Sophia found that she could not induce General Menesius to co-operate with her in any such plans. He had set his heart on making his pupil a virtuous and an accomplished man, and he knew very well that the system of laxity and indulgence which Sophia recommended would end in his ruin. After a considerable contest, Sophia, finding that Menesius was inflexible, manoeuvred to cause him to be dismissed from his office, and to have another arrangement made for the boy, by which she thought her ends would be attained. So Menesius bade his young charge farewell, not, however, without giving him, in parting, most urgent counsels to persevere, as he had begun, in the faithful performance of his duty, to resist every temptation to idleness or excess, and to devote himself, while young, with patience, perseverance, and industry to the work of storing his mind with useful knowledge, and of acquiring every possible art and accomplishment which could be of advantage to him when he became a man.

After General Menesius had been dismissed, Sophia adopted an entirely new system for the management of Peter. Before this time Theodore had died, and Peter, in conjunction with John, had been proclaimed emperor, Sophia governing as regent in their names. The princess now made an arrangement for establishing Peter in a household of his own, at a palace situated in a small village at some distance from Moscow, and she appointed fifty boys to live with him as his playmates and amusers. These boys were provided with every possible means of indulgence, and were subject to very little restraint. The intention of Sophia was that they should do just as they pleased, and she had no doubt that they would spend their time in such a manner that they would all grow up idle, vicious, and good for nothing. There was even some hope that Peter would impair his health to such an extent by excessive indulgences as to bring him to an early grave.

Indeed, the plot was so well contrived that there are probably not many boys who would not, under such circumstances, have fallen into the snare so adroitly laid for them and been ruined; but Peter escaped it. Whether it was from the influence of the counsels and instructions of his former governor, or from his own native good sense, or from both combined, he resisted the temptations that were laid before him, and, instead of giving up his studies, and spending his time in indolence and vice, he improved such privileges as he enjoyed to the best of his ability. He even contrived to turn the hours of play, and the companions who had been given to him as mere instruments of pleasure, into means of improvement. He caused the boys to be organized into a sort of military school, and learned with them all the evolutions, and practiced all the discipline necessary in a camp. He himself began at the very beginning. He caused himself to be taught to drum, not merely as most boys do, just to make a noise for his amusement, but regularly and scientifically, so as to enable him to understand and execute all the beats and signals used in camp and on the field of battle. He studied fortification, and set the boys at work, himself among them, in constructing a battery in a regular and scientific manner. He learned the use of tools, too, practically, in a shop which had been provided for the boys as a place for play; and the wheelbarrow with which he worked in making the fortification was one which he had constructed with his own hands.

He did not assume any superiority over his companions in these exercises, but took his place among them as an equal, obeying the commands which were given to him, when it came to his turn to serve, and taking his full share of all the hardest of the work which was to be done.

Nor was this all mere boys' play, pursued for a little time as long as the novelty lasted, and then thrown aside for something more amusing. Peter knew that when he became a man he would be emperor of all Russia. He knew that among the populations of that immense country there were a great many wild and turbulent tribes, half savage in habits and character, that would never be controlled but by military force, and that the country, too, was surrounded by other nations that would sometimes, unless he was well prepared for them, assume a hostile attitude against his government, and perhaps make great aggressions upon his territories. He wished, therefore, to prepare himself for the emergencies that might in future arise by making himself thoroughly acquainted with all the details of the military art. He did not expect, it is true, that he should ever be called upon to serve in any of his armies as an actual drummer, or to wheel earth and construct fortifications with his own hands, still less to make the wheelbarrows by which the work was to be done; but he was aware that he could superintend these things far more intelligently and successfully if he knew in detail precisely how every thing ought to be done, and that was the reason why he took so much pains to learn himself how to do them.

As he grew older he contrived to introduce higher and higher branches of military art into the school, and to improve and perfect the organization of it in every way. After a while he adopted improved uniforms and equipments for the pupils, such as were used at the military schools of the different nations of Europe; and he established professors of different branches of military science as fast as he himself and his companions advanced in years and in power of appreciating studies more and more elevated. The result was, that when, at length, he was eighteen years of age, and the time arrived for him to leave the place, the institution had become completely established as a well-organized and well-appointed military school, and it continued in successful operation as such for a long time afterward.

It was in a great measure in consequence of the energy and talent which Peter thus displayed that so many of the leading nobles attached themselves to his cause, by which means he was finally enabled to depose Sophia from her regency, and take the power into his own hands, even before he was of age, as related in the last chapter.

CHAPTER IV

LE FORT AND MENZIKOFF

1689-1691

Conditions of success in life—The selection of agents—
Building a house—Secret of success—Peter's youth—Le Fort
and Menzikoff—Merchants of Amsterdam—Le Fort in the
counting-house—He goes to Copenhagen—He becomes
acquainted with military life—The ambassador—Le Fort an
interpreter—He attracts the attention of the emperor—His
judicious answers—Gratification of the emperor—The
embassador's opinion—The glass of wine—Le Fort given up
to the emperor—His appointment at court—His subsequent
career—Uniforms—Le Fort's suggestion—An embassador's
train—Surprise and pleasure of the Czar—Le Fort undertakes
a commission—Making of the uniforms—He enlists a
company—The company appears before the emperor—The
result—New improvements proposed—Changes—
Remodeling of the tariff—Effects of the change—The
finances—Carpenters and masons brought in—New palace—
Le Fort's increasing influence—His generosity—Peter's
violent temper—Le Fort an intercessor—Prince Menzikoff—
His early history—He sets off to seek his fortune—His pies
and cakes—Negotiations with the emperor—Menzikoff in Le
Fort's company—Menzikoff's real character—Quarrel

between Peter and his wife—Cause of the quarrel—Ottokesa's cruel fate—Grave faults in Peter's character

Whatever may be a person's situation in life, his success in his undertakings depends not more, after all, upon his own personal ability to do what is required to be done, than it does upon his sagacity and the soundness of his judgment in selecting the proper persons to co-operate with him and assist him in doing it. In all great enterprises undertaken by men, it is only a very small part which they can execute with their own hands, and multitudes of most excellently contrived plans fail for want of wisdom in the choice of the men who are depended upon for the accomplishment of them.

This is true in all things, small as well as great. A man may form a very wise scheme for building a house. He may choose an excellent place for the location of it, and draw up a good plan, and make ample arrangements for the supply of funds, but if he does not know how to choose, or where to find good builders, his scheme will come to a miserable end. He may choose builders that are competent but dishonest, or they may be honest but incompetent, or they may be subject to some other radical defect; in either of which cases the house will be badly built, and the scheme will be a failure.

Many men say, when such a misfortune as this happens to them, "Ah! it was not my fault. It was the fault of the builders;" to which the proper reply would be, "It *was* your fault. You should not have undertaken to build a house unless, in addition to being able to form the general plan and arrangements wisely, you had also had the sagacity to discern the characters of the men whom you were to employ to execute the work." This latter quality is as important to success in all undertakings as the former. Indeed, it is far more important, for good *men* may correct or avoid the evils of a bad plan, but a good plan can never afford security against the evil action of bad men.

The sovereigns and great military commanders that have acquired the highest celebrity in history have always been remarkable for their tact and sagacity in discovering and bringing forward the right kind of talent for the successful accomplishment of their various designs.

When Peter first found himself nominally in possession of the supreme power, after the fall of the Princess Sophia, he was very young, and the administration of the government was really in the hands of different nobles and officers of state, who managed affairs in his name. From time to time there were great dissensions among these men. They formed themselves into cliques and coteries, each of which was jealous of the influence of the others. As Peter gradually grew older, and felt stronger and stronger in his position, he took a greater part in the direction and control of the public policy, and the persons whom he first made choice of to aid him in his plans were two very able men, whom he afterward raised to positions of great responsibility and honor. These men became, indeed, in the end, highly distinguished as statesmen, and were very prominent and very efficient instruments in the development and realization of Peter's plans. The name of the first of these statesmen was Le Fort; that of the second was Menzikoff. The story which is told by the old historians of both of these men is quite romantic.

Le Fort was the son of a merchant of Geneva. He had a strong desire from his childhood to be a soldier, but his father, considering the hardships and dangers to which a military life would expose him, preferred to make him a merchant, and so he provided him with a place in the counting-house of one of the great merchants of Amsterdam. The city of Amsterdam was in those days one of the greatest and wealthiest marts of commerce in the world.

Very many young men, in being thus restrained by their fathers from pursuing the profession which they themselves chose, and placed, instead, in a situation which they did not like, would have gone to their duty in a discontented and sullen manner, and would have made no effort to succeed in the business or to please their employers; but Le Fort, it seems, was a boy of a different mould from this. He went to his work in the counting-house at Amsterdam with a good heart, and devoted himself to his business with so much industry and steadiness, and evinced withal so much amiableness of disposition in his intercourse with all around him, that before long, as the accounts say, the merchant "loved him as his own child." After some considerable time had elapsed, the merchant, who was constantly sending vessels to different parts of the world, was on one occasion about dispatching a ship to Copenhagen, and Le Fort asked permission to go in her. The merchant was not only willing that he should go, but also gave him the whole charge of the cargo, with instructions to attend to the sale of it, and the remittance of the proceeds on the arrival of the ship in port. Le Fort accordingly sailed in the ship, and on his arrival at Copenhagen he transacted the business of selling the cargo and sending back the money so skillfully and well that the merchant was very well pleased with him.

Copenhagen is the capital of Denmark, and the Danes were at that time quite a powerful and warlike nation. Le Fort, in walking about the streets of the town while his ship was lying there, often saw the Danish soldiers marching to and fro, and performing their evolutions, and the sight revived in his mind his former interest in being a soldier. He soon made acquaintance with some of the officers, and, in hearing them talk of their various adventures, and of the details of their mode of life, he became very eager to join them. They liked him, too, very much. He had made great progress in learning the different languages spoken in that part of the world, and the officers found, moreover, that he was very quick in understanding the military principles which they explained to him, and in learning evolutions of all kinds.

About this time it happened that an embassador was to be sent from Denmark to Russia, and Le Fort, who had a great inclination to see the world as well as to be a soldier, was seized with a strong desire to accompany the expedition in the embassador's train. He already knew something of the Russian language, and he set himself at work with all diligence to study it more. He also obtained recommen-dations from those who had known him—probably, among others, from the merchant in Amsterdam, and he secured the influence in his favor of the officers in Copenhagen with whom he had become acquainted. When these preliminary steps had been taken, he made application for the post of interpreter to the embassy; and after a proper examination had been made in respect to his character and his qualifications, he received the appointment. Thus, instead of going back to Amsterdam after his cargo was sold, he went to Russia in the suite of the embassador.

The embassador soon formed a very strong friendship for his young interpreter, and employed him confidentially, when he arrived in Moscow, in many important services. The embassador himself soon acquired great influence at Moscow, and was admitted to quite familiar intercourse, not only with the leading Russian noblemen, but also with Peter himself. On one occasion, when Peter was dining at the embassador's—as it seems he was sometimes accustomed to do—he took notice of Le Fort, who was present as one of the party, on account of his prepossessing appearance and agreeable manners. He also observed that, for a foreigner, he spoke the Russian language remarkably well. The emperor asked Le Fort some questions concerning his origin and history, and, being very much pleased with his answers, and with his general air and demeanor, he asked him whether he should be willing to enter into his service. Le Fort replied in a very respectful manner, "That, whatever ambition he might have to serve so great a monarch, yet the duty and gratitude which he owed to his present master, the embassador, would not allow him to promise any thing without first asking his consent."

"Very well," replied the Czar; "*I* will ask your master's consent."

"But I hope," said Le Fort, "that your majesty will make use of some other interpreter than myself in asking the question."

Peter was very much pleased with both these answers of Le Fort—the one showing his scrupulous fidelity to his engagements in not being willing to leave one service for another, however advantageous to himself the change might be, until he was honorably released by his first employer, and the other marking the delicacy of mind which prompted him to wish not to take any part in the conversation between the emperor and the embassador respecting himself, as his office of interpreter would naturally lead him to do, but to prefer that the communication should be made through an indifferent person, in order that the embassador might be perfectly free to express his real opinion without any reserve.

Accordingly, the Czar, taking another interpreter with him, went to the embassador and began to ask him about Le Fort.

"He speaks very good Russian," said Peter.

"Yes, please your majesty," said the embassador, "he has a genius for learning any thing that he pleases. When he came

Jacob Abbott

to me four months ago he knew very little of German, but now he speaks it very well. I have two German interpreters in my train, and he speaks the language as well as either of them. He did not know a word of Russian when he came to my country, but your majesty can judge yourself how well he speaks it now."

In the mean time, while Peter and the embassador were talking thus about Le Fort, he himself had withdrawn to another part of the room. The Czar was very much pleased with the modesty of the young gentleman's behavior; and, after finishing the conversation with the embassador, without, however, having asked him to release Le Fort from his service, he returned to the part of the room where Le Fort was, and presently asked him to bring him a glass of wine. He said no more to him at that time in respect to entering his service, but Le Fort understood very well from his countenance, and from the manner in which he asked him for the wine, that nothing had occurred in his conversation with the embassador to lead him to change his mind.

The next day Peter, having probably in the mean time made some farther inquiries about Le Fort, introduced the subject again in conversation with the embassador. He told the embassador that he had a desire to have the young man Le Fort about him, and asked if he should be willing to part with him. The embassador replied that, notwithstanding any desire he might feel to retain so agreeable and promising a man in his own service, still the exchange was too advantageous to Le Fort, and he wished him too well to make any objection to it; and besides, he added, he knew too well his duty to his majesty not to consent readily to any arrangement of that kind that his majesty might desire.

The next day Peter sent for Le Fort, and formally appointed him his first interpreter. The duties of this office required Le

Fort to be a great deal in the emperor's presence, and Peter soon became extremely attached to him. Le Fort, although we have called him a young man, was now about thirty-five years of age, while Peter himself was yet not twenty. It was natural, therefore, that Peter should soon learn to place great confidence in him, and often look to him for information, and this the more readily on account of Le Fort's having been brought up in the heart of Europe, where all the arts of civilization, both those connected with peace and war, were in a much more advanced state than they were at this time in Russia.

Le Fort continued in the service of the emperor until the day of his death, which happened about ten years after this time; and during this period he rose to great distinction, and exercised a very important part in the management of public affairs, and more particularly in aiding Peter to understand and to introduce into his own dominions the arts and improvements of western Europe.

The first improvement which Le Fort was the means of introducing in the affairs of the Czar related to the dress and equipment of the troops. The Guards had before that time been accustomed to wear an old-fashioned Russian uniform, which was far from being convenient. The outside garment was a sort of long coat or gown, which considerably impeded the motion of the limbs. One day, not long after Le Fort entered the service of the emperor, Peter, being engaged in conversation with him, asked him what he thought of his soldiers.

"The men themselves are very well," replied Le Port, "but it seems to me that the dress which they wear is not so convenient for military use as the style of dress now usually adopted among the western nations."

Peter asked what this style was, and Le Fort replied that if his majesty would permit him to do so, he would take measures for affording him an opportunity to see.

Accordingly, Le Fort repaired immediately to the tailor of the Danish embassador. This tailor the embassador had brought with him from Copenhagen, for it was the custom in those days for personages of high rank and station, like the embassador, to take with them, in their train, persons of all the trades and professions which they might require, so that, wherever they might be, they could have the means of supplying all their wants within themselves, and without at all depending upon the people whom they visited. Le Fort employed the tailor to make him two military suits, in the style worn by the royal guards at Copenhagen—one for an officer, and another for a soldier of the ranks. The tailor finished the first suit in two days. Le Fort put the dress on, and in the morning, at the time when, according to his usual custom, he was to wait upon the emperor in his chamber, he went in wearing the new uniform.

The Czar was surprised at the unexpected spectacle. At first he did not know Le Fort in his new garb; and when at length he recognized him, and began to understand the case, he was exceedingly pleased. He examined the uniform in every part, and praised not only the dress itself, but also Le Fort's ingenuity and diligence in procuring him so good an opportunity to know what the military style of the western nations really was.

Soon after this Le Fort appeared again in the emperor's presence wearing the uniform of a common soldier. The emperor examined this dress too, and saw the superiority of it in respect to its convenience, and its adaptedness to the wants and emergencies of military life. He said at once that he should like to have a company of guards dressed and equipped in that manner, and should be also very much pleased to have them disciplined and drilled according to the western style. Le Fort said that if his majesty was pleased to intrust him with the commission, he would endeavor to organize such a company.

The emperor requested him to do so, and Le Port immediately undertook the task. He went about Moscow to all the different merchants to procure the materials necessary—for many of these materials were such as were not much in use in Moscow, and so it was not easy to procure them in sufficient quantities to make the number of suits that Le Fort required. He also sought out all the tailors that he could find at the houses of the different embassadors, or of the great merchants who came from western Europe, and were consequently acquainted with the mode of cutting and making the dresses in the proper manner. Of course, a considerable number of tailors would be necessary to make up so many uniforms in the short space of time which Le Fort wished to allot to the work.

Le Fort then went about among the strangers and foreigners at Moscow, both those connected with the embassadors and others, to find men that were in some degree acquainted with the drill and tactics of the western armies, who were willing to serve in the company that he was about to organize. He soon made up a company of fifty men. When this company was completed, and clothed in the new uniform, and had been properly drilled, Le Fort put himself at the head of them one morning, and marched them, with drums beating and colors flying, before the palace gate. The Czar came to the window to see them as they passed. He was much surprised at the spectacle, and very much pleased. He came down to look at the men more closely; he stood by while they went through the exercises in which Le Fort had drilled them. The emperor was so much pleased that he said he would join the company himself. He wished to learn to perform the exercise personally, so as to know in a practical manner precisely how others ought to perform it. He accordingly caused a dress to be made for himself, and he took his place afterward in the ranks as a common soldier, and was drilled with the rest in all the exercises.

From this beginning the change went on until the style of dress and the system of tactics for the whole imperial army was reformed by the introduction of the compact and scientific system of western Europe, in the place of the old-fashioned and cumbrous usages which had previously prevailed.

The emperor having experienced the immense advantages which resulted from the adoption of western improvements in his army, wished now to make an experiment of introducing, in the same way, the elements of western civilization into the ordinary branches of industry and art. He proposed to Le Fort to make arrangements for bringing into the country a great number of mechanics and artisans from Denmark, Germany, France, and other European countries, in order that their improved methods and processes might be introduced into Russia. Le Fort readily entered into this proposal, but he explained to the emperor that, in order to render such a measure successful on the scale necessary for the accomplishment of any important good, it would be first requisite to make some considerable changes in the general laws of the land, especially in relation to intercourse with foreign nations. On his making known fully and in detail what these changes would be, the emperor readily acceded to them, and the proposed modifications of the laws were made. The tariff of duties on the products and manufactures of foreign countries was greatly reduced. This produced a two-fold effect.

In the first place, it greatly increased the importations of goods from foreign countries, and thus promoted the intercourse of the Russians with foreign merchants, manufacturers, and artisans, and gradually accustomed the people to a better style of living, and to improved fashions in dress, furniture, and equipage, and thus prepared the country to furnish an extensive market for the encouragement of Russian arts and manufactures as fast as they could be introduced.

In the second place, the new system greatly increased the revenues of the empire. It is true that the tariff was reduced, so that the articles that were imported paid only about half as much in proportion after the change as before. But then the new laws increased the importations so much, that the loss was very much more than made up to the treasury, and the emperor found in a very short time that the state of his finances was greatly improved. This enabled him to take measures for introducing into the country great numbers of foreign manufacturers and artisans from Germany, France, Scotland, and other countries of western Europe. These men were brought into the country by the emperor, and sustained there at the public expense, until they had become so far established in their several professions and trades that they could maintain themselves. Among others, he brought in a great many carpenters and masons to teach the Russians to build better habitations than those which they had been accustomed to content themselves with, which were, in general, wooden huts of very rude and inconvenient construction. One of the first undertakings in which the masons were employed was the building of a handsome palace of hewn stone in Moscow for the emperor himself, the first edifice of that kind which had ever been built in that city. The sight of a palace formed of so elegant and durable a material excited the emulation of all the wealthy noblemen, so that, as soon as the masons were released from their engagement with the emperor, they found plenty of employment in building new houses and palaces for these noblemen.

These and a great many other similar measures were devised by Le Fort during the time that he continued in the service of the Czar, and the success which attended all his plans and proposals gave him, in the end, great influence, and was the means of acquiring for him great credit and renown. And yet he was so discreet and unpretending in his manners and demeanor, if the accounts which have come down to us respecting him are correct, that the high favor in which he was held by the emperor did not awaken in the hearts of the native nobles of the land any considerable degree of that jealousy and ill-will which they might have been expected to excite. Le Fort was of a very self-sacrificing and disinterested disposition. He was generous in his dealings with all, and he often exerted the ascendency which he had acquired over the mind of the emperor to save other officers from undeserved or excessive punishment when they displeased their august master; for it must be confessed that Peter, notwithstanding all the excellences of his character, had the reputation at this period of his life of being hasty and passionate. He was very impatient of contradiction, and he could not tolerate any species of opposition to his wishes. Being possessed himself of great decision of character, and delighting, as he did, in promptness and energy of action, he lost all patience sometimes, when annoyed by the delays, or the hesitation, or the inefficiency of others, who were not so richly endowed by nature as himself. In these cases he was often unreasonable, and sometimes violent; and he would in many instances have acted in an ungenerous and cruel manner if Le Fort had not always been at hand to restrain and appease him.

Le Fort always acted as intercessor in cases of difficulty of this sort; so that the Russian noblemen, or boyars as they were called, in the end looked upon him as their father. It is said that he actually saved the lives of great numbers of them, whom Peter, without his intercession, would have sentenced to death. Others he saved from the knout, and others from banishment. At one time, when the emperor in a passion, was going to cause one of his officers to be scourged, although, as Le Fort thought, he had been guilty of no wrong which could deserve such a punishment, Le Fort, after all other means had failed, bared his own breast and shoulders, and bade the angry emperor to strike or cut there if he would, but to spare the innocent person. The Czar was entirely overcome by this noble generosity, and, clasping Le Fort in his arms, thanked him for his interposition, at the same time allowing the trembling prisoner to depart in peace, with his heart full of gratitude toward the friend who had so nobly saved him.

Another of the chief officers in Peter's service during the early part of his reign was the Prince Menzikoff. His origin was very humble. His Christian name was Alexander, and his father was a laboring man in the service of a monastery on the banks of the Volga. The monasteries of those times were endowed with large tracts of valuable land, which were cultivated by servants or vassals, and from the proceeds of this cultivation the monks were supported, and the monastery buildings kept in repair or enlarged.

Alexander spent the early years of his life in working with his father on the monastery lands; but, being a lad of great spirit and energy, he gradually became dissatisfied with this mode of life; for the peasants of those days, such as his father, who tilled the lands of the nobles or of the monks, were little better than slaves. Alexander, then, when he arrived at the age of thirteen or fourteen, finding his situation and prospects at home very gloomy and discouraging, concluded to go out into the world and seek his fortune.

So he left his father's hut and set out for Moscow. After meeting with various adventures on the way and in the city, he finally found a place in a pastry-cook's shop; but, instead of being employed in making and baking the pies and tarts, he was sent out into the streets to sell them. In order to attract customers to his merchandise, he used to sing songs and tell stories in the streets. Indeed, it was the talent which he evinced in these arts, doubtless, which led his master to employ him in this way, instead of keeping him at work at home in the baking.

The story which is told of the manner in which the emperor's attention was first attracted to young Menzikoff is very curious, but, as is the case with all other such personal anecdotes related of great sovereigns, it is very doubtful how far it is to be believed. It is said that Peter, passing along the street one day, stopped to listen to Menzikoff as he was singing a song or telling a story to a crowd of listeners. He was much diverted by one of the songs that he heard, and at the close of it he spoke to the boy, and finally asked him what he would take for his whole stock of cakes and pies, basket and all. The boy named the sum for which he would sell all the cakes and pies, but as for the basket he said that belonged to his master, and he had no power to sell it.

"Still," he added, "every thing belongs to your majesty, and your majesty has, therefore, only to give me the command, and I shall deliver it up to you."

This reply pleased the Czar so much that he sent for the boy to come to him, and on conversing with him farther, and after making additional inquiries respecting him, he was so well satisfied that he took him at once into his service.

All this took place before Le Fort's plan was formed for organizing a company to exhibit to the emperor the style of uniform and the system of military discipline adopted in western Europe, as has already been described. Menzikoff joined this company, and he took so much interest in the exercises and evolutions, and evinced so great a degree of intelligence, and so much readiness in comprehending and in practicing the various manoeuvres, that he attracted Le Fort's special attention. He was soon promoted to office in the company, and ultimately he became Le Fort's principal co-operator in his various measures and plans. From this he rose by degrees, until in process of time he became one of the most distinguished generals in Peter's army, and took a very important part in some of his most celebrated campaigns.

In reading stories like these, we are naturally led to feel a strong interest in the persons who are the subjects of them, and we sometimes insensibly form opinions of their characters which are far too favorable. This Menzikoff, for example, notwithstanding the enterprising spirit which he displayed in his boyhood, in setting off alone to Moscow to seek his fortune, and his talent for telling stories and singing songs, and the interest which he felt, and the success that he met with, in learning Le Fort's military manoeuvres, and the great distinction which he subsequently acquired as a military commander, may have been, after all, in relation to any just and proper standards of moral duty, a very bad man. Indeed, there is much reason to suppose that he was so. At all events, he became subsequently implicated in a dreadful quarrel which took place between Peter and his wife, under circumstances which appear very much against him. This quarrel occurred after Peter had been married only about two years, and when he was yet not quite twenty years old. As usual in such cases, very different stories are told by the friends respectively of the husband and the wife. On the part of the empress it was said that the difficulty arose from

Peter's having been drawn away into bad company, and especially the company of bad women, through the instrumentality of Menzikoff when he first came into Peter's service. Menzikoff was a dissolute young man, it was said, while he was in the service of the pastry-cook, and was accustomed to frequent the haunts of the vicious and depraved about the town; and after he entered into Peter's service, Peter himself began to go with him to these places, disguised, of course, so as not to be known. This troubled Ottokesa, and made her jealous; and when she remonstrated with her husband he was angry, and by way of recrimination accused her of being unfaithful to him. Menzikoff too was naturally filled with resentment at the empress's accusations against him, and he took Peter's part against his wife. Whatever may have been the truth in regard to the grounds of the complaints made by the parties against each other, the power was on Peter's side. He repudiated his wife, and then shut her up in a place of seclusion, where he kept her confined all the remainder of her days.

Besides the unfavorable inferences which we might justly draw from this case, there are unfortunately other indications that Peter, notwithstanding the many and great excellences of his character, was at this period of his life violent and passionate in temper, very impatient of contradiction or opposition, and often unreasonable and unjust in his treatment of those who for any reason became the objects of his suspicion or dislike. Various incidents and occurrences illustrating these traits in his character will appear in the subsequent chapters of his history.

CHAPTER V

COMMENCEMENT OF THE REIGN

1691-1697

Peter's unlimited power—Extent of his dominions—
Character—His wishes in respect to his dominion—Embassy
to China—Siberia—Inhospitable climate—The exiles—
Western civilization—Ship-building—The Dutch ship-yards
—Saardam—The barge at the country palace—The
emperor's first vessels—Sham-fights—Azof—Naval
operations against Azof—Treachery of the artilleryman—
Defeat—New attempt—The Turkish fleet taken—Fall of
Azof—Fame of the emperor—His plans for building a
fleet—Foreign workmen—Penalties—His arbitrary
proceedings—He sends the young nobility abroad—
Opposition—Sullen mood of mind—National prejudices
offended—The opposition party—Arguments of the
disaffected—Religious feelings of the people—The patriarch
—An impious scheme—Plan of the conspirators—Fires—
Dread of them in Moscow—Modern cities—Plan for
massacring the foreigners—The day—The plot revealed—
Measures taken by Peter—Torture—Punishment of the
conspirators—The column in the market-place

Peter was now not far from twenty years of age, and he was

Jacob Abbott

in full possession of power as vast, perhaps—if we consider both the extent of it and its absoluteness—as was ever claimed by any European sovereign. There was no written constitution to limit his prerogatives, and no Legislature or Parliament to control him by laws. In a certain sense, as Alexander Menzikoff said when selling his cakes, every thing belonged to him. His word was law. Life and death hung upon his decree. His dominions extended so far that, on an occasion when he wished to send an embassador to one of his neighbors—the Emperor of China—it took the messenger more than *eighteen months* of constant and diligent traveling to go from the capital to the frontier.

Such was Peter's position. As to character, he was talented, ambitious, far-seeing, and resolute; but he was also violent in temper, merciless and implacable toward his enemies, and possessed of an indomitable will.

He began immediately to feel a strong interest in the improvement of his empire, in order to increase his own power and grandeur as the monarch of it, just as a private citizen might wish to improve his estate in order to increase his wealth and importance as the owner of it. He sent the embassador above referred to to China in order to make arrangements for increasing and improving the trade between the two countries. This mission was arranged in a very imposing manner. The embassador was attended with a train of twenty-one persons, who went with him in the capacity of secretaries, interpreters, legal councilors, and the like, besides a large number of servants and followers to wait upon the gentlemen of the party, and to convey and take care of the baggage. The baggage was borne in a train of wagons which followed the carriages of the embassador and his suite, so that the expedition moved through the country quite like a little army on a march.

It was nearly three years before the embassage returned. The measure, however, was eminently successful. It placed the relations of the two empires on a very satisfactory footing.

The dominions of the Czar extended then, as now, through all the northern portions of Europe and Asia, to the shores of the Icy Sea. A very important part of this region is the famous Siberia. The land here is not of much value for cultivation, on account of the long and dreary winters and the consequent shortness of the summer season. But this very coldness of the climate causes it to produce a great number of fine fur-bearing animals, such as the sable, the mink, the ermine, and the otter; for nature has so arranged it that, the colder any climate is, the finer and the warmer is the fur which grows upon the animals that live there.

The inhabitants of Siberia are employed, therefore, chiefly in hunting wild animals for their flesh or their fur, and in working the mines; and, from time immemorial, it has been the custom to send criminals there in banishment, and compel them to spend the remainder of their lives in these toilsome and dangerous occupations. Of course, the cold, the exposure, and the fatigue, joined to the mental distress and suffering which the thought of their hard fate and the recollections of home must occasion, soon bring far the greater proportion of these unhappy outcasts to the grave.

Peter interested himself very much in efforts to open communications with these retired and almost inaccessible regions, and to improve and extend the working of the mines. But his thoughts were chiefly occupied with the condition of the European portion of his dominions, and with schemes for introducing more and more fully the arts and improvements of western Europe among his people. He was ready to seize upon every occasion which could furnish any hint or suggestion to this end.

The manner in which his attention was first turned to the subject of ship-building illustrated this. In those days Holland was the great centre of commerce and navigation for the whole world, and the art of ship-building had made more progress in that nation than in any other. The Dutch held colonies in every quarter of the globe. Their men-of-war and their fleets of merchantmen penetrated to every sea, and their naval commanders were universally renowned for their enterprise, their bravery, and their nautical skill.

The Dutch not only built ships for themselves, but orders were sent to their ship-yards from all parts of the world, inasmuch as in these yards all sorts of vessels, whether for war, commerce, or pleasure, could be built better and cheaper than in any other place.

One of the chief centres in which these ship and boat building operations were carried on was the town of Saardam. This town lies near Amsterdam, the great commercial capital of the country. It extends for a mile or two along the banks of a deep and still river, which furnish most complete and extensive facilities for the docks and ship-yards.

Now it happened that, one day when Peter was with Le Fort at one of his country palaces where there was a little lake, and a canal connected with it, which had been made for pleasure-sailing on the grounds, his attention was attracted to the form and construction of a yacht which was lying there. This yacht having been sent for from Holland at the time when the palace grounds were laid out, the emperor fell into conversation with Le Fort in respect to it, and this led to the subject of ships and ship-building in general. Le Fort represented so strongly to his master the advantages which Holland and the other maritime powers of Europe derived from their ships of war, that Peter began immediately to feel a strong desire to possess a navy himself. There were, of course, great difficulties in the way. Russia was almost entirely an inland country. There were no good sea-ports, and Moscow, the capital, was situated very far in the interior. Then, besides, Peter not only had no ships, but there were no mechanics or artisans in Russia that knew how to build them.

Le Fort, however, when he perceived how deep was the interest which Peter felt in the subject, made inquiries, and at length succeeded in finding among the Dutch merchants that were in Moscow the means of procuring some ship-builders to build him several small vessels, which, when they were completed, were launched upon a lake not far from the city. Afterward other vessels were built in the same place, in the form of frigates; and these, when they were launched, were properly equipped and armed, under Le Fort's direction, and the emperor took great interest in sailing about in them on the lake, in learning personally all the evolutions necessary for the management of them, and in performing sham-fights by setting one of them against another. He took command of one of the vessels as captain, and thenceforward assumed that designation as one of his most honorable titles. All this took place when Peter was about twenty-two years old.

Not very long after this the emperor had an opportunity to make a commencement in converting his nautical knowledge to actual use by engaging in something like a naval operation against an enemy, in conjunction with several other European powers, he declared war anew against the Turks and Tartars, and the chief object of the first campaign was the capture of the city of Azof, which is situated on the shores of the Sea of Azof, near the mouth of the River Don. Peter not only approached and invested the city by land, but he also took possession of the river leading to it by means of a great number of boats and vessels which he caused to be built along the banks. In this way he cut off all supplies from the city, and pressed it so closely that he would have taken it, it was said, had it not been for the treachery of an officer of artillery, who betrayed to the enemy the principal battery which had been raised against the town just as it was ready to be opened upon the walls. This artilleryman, who was not a native Russian, but one of the foreigners whom the Czar had enlisted in his service, became exasperated at some ill treatment which he received from the Russian nobleman who commanded his corps; so he secretly drove nails into the touchholes of all the guns in the battery, and then, in the night, went over to the Turks and informed them what he had done. Accordingly, very early in the morning the Turks sallied forth and attacked the battery, and the men who were charged with the defense of it, on rushing to the guns, found that they could not be fired. The consequence was that the battery was taken, the men put to flight, and the guns destroyed. This defeat entirely disconcerted the Russian army, and so effectually deranged their plans that they were obliged to raise the siege and withdraw, with the expectation, however, of renewing the attempt in another campaign.

Accordingly, the next year the attempt was renewed, and many more boats and vessels were built upon the river to co-operate with the besiegers. The Turks had ships of their own, which they brought into the Sea of Azof for the protection of the town. But Peter sent down a few of his smaller vessels, and by means of them contrived to entice the Turkish commander up a little way into the river. Peter then came down upon him with all his fleet, and the Turkish ships were overpowered and taken. Thus Peter gained his first naval victory almost, as we might say, on the land. He conquered and captured a fleet of sea-going ships by enticing them among the boats and other small craft which he had built up country on the banks of a river.

Soon after this Azof was taken. One of the conditions of the surrender was that the treacherous artilleryman should be delivered up to the Czar. He was taken to Moscow, and there put to death with tortures too horrible to be described. They did not deny that the man had been greatly injured by his Russian commander, but they told him that what he ought to have done was to appeal to the emperor for redress, and not to seek his revenge by traitorously giving up to the enemy the trust committed to his charge.

The emperor acquired great fame throughout Europe by the success of his operations in the siege of Azof. This success also greatly increased his interest in the building of ships, especially as he now, since Azof had fallen into his hands, had a port upon an open sea.

In a word, Peter was now very eager to begin at once the building ships of war. He was determined that he would have a fleet which would enable him to go out and meet the Turks in the Black Sea. The great difficulty was to provide the necessary funds. To accomplish this purpose, Peter, who was never at all scrupulous in respect to the means which he adopted for attaining his ends, resorted at once to very decided measures. Besides the usual taxes which were laid upon the people to maintain the war, he ordained that a certain number of wealthy noblemen should each pay for one ship, which, however, as some compensation for the cost which the nobleman was put to in building it, he was at liberty to call by his own name. The same decree was made in respect to a number of towns, monasteries, companies, and public institutions. The emperor also made arrangements for having a large number of workmen sent into Russia from Holland, and from Venice, and from other maritime countries. The emperor laid his plans in this way for the construction and equipment of a fleet of about one hundred ships and vessels, consisting of frigates, store-ships, bomb-vessels, galleys, and galliasses. These were all to be built, equipped, and made in all respects ready for sea in the space of three years; and if any person or party failed to have his ship ready at that time, the amount of the tax which had been assessed to him was to be doubled.

In all these proceedings, the Czar, as might have been expected from his youth and his headstrong character, acted in a very summary, and in many respects in an arbitrary and despotic manner. His decrees requiring the nobles to contribute such large sums for the building of his fleet occasioned a great deal of dissatisfaction and complaint. And very soon he resorted to some other measures, which increased the general discontent exceedingly.

He appointed a considerable number of the younger nobility, and the sons of other persons of wealth and distinction, to travel in the western countries of Europe while the fleet was preparing, giving them special instructions in respect to the objects of interest which they should severally examine and study. The purpose of this measure was to advance the general standard of intelligence in Russia by affording to these young men the advantages of foreign travel, and enlarging their ideas in respect to the future progress of their own country in the arts and appliances of civilized life. The general idea of the emperor in this was excellent, and the effect of the measure would have been excellent too if it had been carried out in a more gentle and moderate way. But the fathers of the young men were incensed at having their sons ordered thus peremptorily out of the country, whether they liked to go or not, and however inconvenient it might be for the fathers to provide the large amounts of money which were required for such journeys. It is said that one young man was so angry at being thus sent away that he determined that his country should not derive any benefit from the measure, so far as his case was concerned, and accordingly, when he arrived at Venice, which was the place where he was sent, he shut himself up in his house, and remained there all the time, in order that he might not see or learn any thing to make use of on his return.

This seems almost incredible. Indeed, the story has more the air of a witticism, invented to express the sullen humor with which many of the young men went away, than the sober statement of a fact. Still, it is not impossible that such a thing may have actually occurred; for the veneration of the old Russian families for their own country, and the contempt with which they had been accustomed for many generations to look upon foreigners, and upon every thing connected with foreign manners and customs, were such as might lead in extreme cases, to almost any degree of fanaticism in resisting the emperor's measures. At any rate, in a short time there was quite a powerful party formed in opposition to the foreign influences which Peter was introducing into the country.

There was no one in the imperial family to whom this party could look for a leader and head except the Princess Sophia. The Czar John, Peter's feeble brother, was dead, otherwise they might have made his name their rallying cry. Sophia was still shut up in the convent to which Peter had sent her on the discovery of her conspiracy against him. She was kept very closely guarded there. Still, the leaders of the opposition contrived to open a communication with her. They took every means to increase and extend the prevailing discontent. To people of wealth and rank they represented the heavy taxes which they were obliged to pay to defray the expenses of the emperor's wild schemes, and the loss of their own proper influence and power in the government of the country, they themselves being displaced to make room for foreigners, or favorites like Menzikoff, that were raised from the lowest grades of life to posts of honor and profit which ought to be bestowed upon the ancient nobility alone. To the poor and ignorant they advanced other arguments, which were addressed chiefly to their religious prejudices. The government were subverting all the ancient usages of the country, they said, and throwing every thing into the hands of infidel or heretical foreigners. The course which the Czar was pursuing was contrary to the laws of God, they said, who had forbidden the children of Israel to have any communion with the unbelieving nations around them, in order that they might not be led away by them into idolatry. And so in Russia, they said, the extensive power of granting permission to any Russian subject to leave the country vested, according to the ancient usages of the empire, with the patriarch, the head of the Church—and Peter had violated these usages in sending away so many of the sons of the nobility without the patriarch's consent. There were many other measures, too, which Peter had adopted, or which he had then in contemplation, that were equally obnoxious to the charge of impiety. For instance, he had formed a plan—and he had even employed engineers to take preliminary steps in reference to the execution of it—for making a canal from the River Wolga to the River Don, thus presumptuously and impiously undertaking to turn the streams one way, when Providence had designed them to flow in another! Absurd as many of these representations were, they had great influence with the mass of the common people.

At length this opposition party became so extended and so strong that the leaders thought the time had arrived for them to act. They accordingly arranged the details of their plot, and prepared to put it in execution.

The scheme which they formed was this: they were to set fire to some houses in the night, not far from the royal palace, and when the emperor came out, as it is said was his custom to do, in order to assist in extinguishing the flames, they were to set upon him and assassinate him.

It may seem strange that it should be the custom of the emperor himself to go out and assist personally in extinguishing fires. But it so happened that the houses of Moscow at this time were almost all built of wood, and they were so combustible, and were, moreover, so much exposed, on account of the many fires required in the winter season in so cold a climate, that the city was subject to dreadful conflagrations. So great was the danger, that the inhabitants were continually in dread of it, and all classes vied with each other in efforts to avert the threatened calamity whenever a fire broke out. Besides this, there were in those days no engines for throwing water, and no organized department of firemen. All this, of course, is entirely different at the present day in modern cities, where houses are built of brick or stone, and the arrangements for extinguishing fires are so complete that an alarm of fire creates no sensation, but people go on with their business or saunter carelessly along the streets, while the firemen are gathering, without feeling the least concern.

As soon as they had made sure of the death of the Czar, the conspirators were to repair to the convent where Sophia was imprisoned, release her from her confinement, and proclaim her queen. They were then to reorganize the Guards, restore all the officers who had been degraded at the time of Couvansky's rebellion, then massacre all the foreigners whom Peter had brought into the country, especially his particular favorites, and so put every thing back upon its ancient footing.

The time fixed for the execution of this plot was the night of the 2d of February, 1697; but the whole scheme was defeated by what the conspirators would probably call the treachery of two of their number. These were two officers of the Guards who had been concerned in the plot, but whose hearts failed them when the hour arrived for putting it into execution.

Falling into conversation with each other just before the time, and finding that they agreed in feeling on the subject, they resolved at once to go and make a full confession to the Czar.

So they went immediately to the house of Le Fort, where the Czar then was, and made a confession of the whole affair. They related all the details of the plot, and gave the names of the principal persons concerned in it.

The emperor was at table with Le Fort at the time that he received this communication. He listened to it very coolly—manifested no surprise—but simply rose from the table, ordered a small body of men to attend him, and, taking the names of the principal conspirators, he went at once to their several houses and arrested them on the spot.

The leaders having been thus seized, the execution of the plot was defeated. The prisoners were soon afterward put to the torture, in order to compel them to confess their crime, and to reveal the names of all their confederates. Whether the names thus extorted from them by suffering were false or true would of course be wholly uncertain, but all whom they named were seized, and, after a brief and very informal trial, all, or nearly all, were condemned to death. The sentence of death was executed on them in the most barbarous manner. A great column was erected in the market-place in Moscow, and fitted with iron spikes and hooks, which were made to project from it on every side, from top to bottom. The criminals were then brought out one by one, and first their arms were cut off, then their legs, and finally their heads. The amputated limbs were then hung up upon the column by the hooks, and the heads were fixed to the spikes. There they remained—a horrid spectacle, intended to strike terror into all beholders—through February and March, as long as the weather continued cold enough to keep them frozen. When at length the spring came on, and the flesh of these dreadful trophies began to thaw, they were taken down and thrown together into a pit, among the bodies of common thieves and murderers.

This was the end of the second conspiracy formed against the life of Peter the Great.

CHAPTER VI

THE EMPEROR'S TOUR

1697

Objects of the tour—An embassy to be sent—The emperor to go incognito—His associates—The regency—Disposition of the Guards—The embassy leaves Moscow—Riga—Not allowed to see the fortifications—Arrival at Konigsberg—Grand procession in entering the city—The pages—Curiosity of the people—The escort—Crowds in the streets—The embassy arrives at its lodgings—Audience of the king—Presents—Delivery of the letter from the Czar—Its contents—The king's reply—Grand banquet—Effects of such an embassy—The policy of modern governments—The people now reserve their earnings for their own use—How Peter occupied his time—Dantzic—Peter preserves his incognito—Presents—His dress—His interest in the shipping—Grand entrance into Holland—Curiosity of the people—Peter enters Amsterdam privately—Views of the Hollanders—Residence of the Czar—The East India Company—Peter goes to work—His real object in pursuing this course—His taste for mechanics—The opportunities and facilities he enjoyed—His old workshop—Mode of preserving it—The workmen in the yard—Peter's visits to his friends in Amsterdam—The rich merchant—Peter's manners

At the time when the emperor issued his orders to so many of the sons of the nobility, requiring them to go and reside for a time in the cities of western Europe, he formed the design of going himself to make a tour in that part of the world, for the purpose of visiting the courts and capitals, and seeing with his own eyes what arts and improvements were to be found there which might be advantageously introduced into his own dominions. In the spring of the year 1697, he thought that the time had come for carrying this idea into effect.

The plan which he formed was not to travel openly in his own name, for he knew that in this case a great portion of his time and attention, in the different courts and capitals, would be wasted in the grand parades, processions, and ceremonies with which the different sovereigns would doubtless endeavor to honor his visit. He therefore determined to travel incognito, in the character of a private person in the train of an embassy. An embassy could proceed more quietly from place to place than a monarch traveling in his own name; and then besides, if the emperor occupied only a subordinate place in the train of the embassy, he could slip away from it to pursue his own inquiries in a private manner whenever he pleased, leaving the embassadors themselves and those of their train who enjoyed such scenes to go through all the public receptions and other pompous formalities which would have been so tiresome to him.

General Le Fort, who had by this time been raised to a very high position under Peter's government, was placed at the head of this embassy. Two other great officers of state were associated with him. Then came secretaries, interpreters, and subordinates of all kinds, in great numbers, among whom Peter was himself enrolled under a fictitious name. Peter

Jacob Abbott

took with him several young men of about his own age. Two or three of these were particular friends of his, whom he wished to have accompany him for the sake of their companionship on the journey. There were some others whom he selected on account of the talent which they had evinced for mechanical and mathematical studies. These young men he intended to have instructed in the art of ship-building in some of the countries which the embassy were to visit.

Besides these arrangements in respect to the embassy, provision was, of course, to be made by the emperor for the government of the country during his absence. He left the administration in the hands of three great nobles, the first of whom was one of his uncles, his mother's brother. The name of this prince was Naraskin. The other two nobles were associated with Naraskin in the regency. These commissioners were to have the whole charge of the government of the country during the Czar's absence. Peter's little son, whose name was Alexis, and who was now about seven years old, was also committed to their keeping.

Not having entire confidence in the fidelity of the old Guards, Peter did not trust the defense of Moscow to them, but he garrisoned the fortifications in and around the capital with a force of about twelve thousand men that he had gradually brought together for that purpose. A great many of these troops, both officers and men, were foreigners. Peter placed greater reliance on them on that account, supposing that they would be less likely to sympathize with and join the people of the city in case of any popular discontent or disturbances. The Guards were sent off into the interior and toward the frontiers, where they could do no great mischief; even if disposed.

At length, when every thing was ready, the embassy set out

from Moscow. The departure of the expedition from the gates of the city made quite an imposing scene, so numerous was the party which composed the embassadors' train. There were in all about three hundred men. The principal persons of the embassy were, of course, splendidly mounted and equipped, and they were followed by a line of wagons conveying supplies of clothing, stores, presents for foreign courts, and other baggage. This baggage-train was, of course, attended by a suitable escort. Vast multitudes of people assembled along the streets and at the gates of the city to see the grand procession commence its march.

The first place of importance at which the embassy stopped was the city of Riga, on the shores of the Gulf of Riga, in the eastern part of the Baltic Sea.[1] Riga and the province in which it was situated, though now a part of the Russian empire, then belonged to Sweden. It was the principal port on the Baltic in those days, and Peter felt a great interest in viewing it, as there was then no naval outlet in that direction from his dominions. The governor of Riga was very polite to the embassy, and gave them a very honorable reception in the city, but he refused to allow the embassadors to examine the fortifications. It had been arranged beforehand between the embassadors and Peter that two of them were to ask permission to see the fortifications, and that Peter himself was to go around with them as their attendant when they made their visit, in order that he might make his own observations in respect to the strength of the works and the mode of their construction. Peter was accordingly very much disappointed and vexed at the refusal of the governor to allow the fortifications to be viewed, and he secretly resolved that he would seize the first opportunity after his return to open a quarrel with the King of Sweden, and take this city away from him.

Leaving Riga, the embassy moved on toward the southward

Jacob Abbott

and westward until, at length, they entered the dominions of the King of Prussia. They came soon to the city of Konigsberg, which was at that time the capital. The reception of the embassy at this city was attended with great pomp and display. The whole party halted at a small village at the distance of about a mile from the gates, in order to give time for completing the arrangements, and to await the arrival of a special messenger and an escort from the king to conduct them within the walls.

At length, when all was ready, the procession formed about four o'clock in the afternoon. First came a troop of horses that belonged to the king. They were splendidly caparisoned, but were not mounted. They were led by grooms. Then came an escort of troops of the Royal Guards. They were dressed in splendid red uniform, and were preceded by kettle-drums. Then a company of the Prussian nobility in beautifully-decorated coaches, each drawn by six horses. Next came the state carriages of the king. The king himself was not in either of them, it being etiquette for the king to remain in his palace, and receive the embassy at a public audience there after their arrival. The royal carriages were sent out, however, as a special though indirect token of respect to the Czar, who was known to be in the train.

Then came a precession of pages, consisting of those of the king and those of the embassadors marching together. These pages were all beautiful boys, elegantly dressed in characteristic liveries of red laced with gold. They marched three together, two of the king's pages in each rank, with one of the embassadors' between them. The spectators were very much interested in these boys, and the boys were likewise doubtless much interested in each other; but they could not hold any conversation with each other, for probably those of each set could speak only their own language.

Next after the pages came the embassy itself. First there was a line of thirty-six carriages, containing the principal officers and attendants of the three embassadors. In one of these carriages, riding quietly with the rest as a subordinate in the train, was Peter. There was doubtless some vague intimation circulating among the crowd that the Emperor of Russia was somewhere in the procession, concealed in his disguise. But there were no means of identifying him, and, of course, whatever curiosity the people felt on the subject remained ungratified.

Next after these carriages came the military escort which the embassadors had brought with them. The escort was headed by the embassadors' band of music, consisting of trumpets, kettle-drums, and other martial instruments. Then came a body of foot-guards: their uniform was green, and they were armed with silver battle-axes. Then came a troop of horsemen, which completed the escort. Immediately after the escort there followed the grand state carriage of the embassy, with the three embassadors in it.

The procession was closed by a long train of elegant carriages, conveying various personages of wealth and distinction, who had come from the city to join in doing honor to the strangers.

As the procession entered the city, they found the streets through which they were to pass densely lined on each side by the citizens who had assembled to witness the spectacle. Through this vast concourse the embassadors and their suite advanced, and were finally conducted to a splendid palace which had been prepared for them in the heart of the city. The garrison of the city was drawn up at the gates of the palace, to receive them as they arrived. When the carriage reached the gate and the embassadors began to alight, a grand salute was fired from the guns of the fortress. The embassadors were immediately conducted to their several apartments in the palace by the officers who had led the procession, and then left to repose. When the officers were about to withdraw, the embassadors accompanied them to the head of the stairs and took leave of them there. The doors of the palace and the halls and entrances leading to the apartments of the embassadors were guarded by twenty-four soldiers, who were stationed there as sentinels to protect the precincts from all intrusion.

Four days after this there was another display, when the embassadors were admitted to their first public audience with the king. There was again a grand procession through the streets, with great crowds assembled to witness it, and bands of music, and splendid uniforms, and gorgeous equipages, all more magnificent, if possible, than before. The embassadors were conducted in this way to the royal palace. They entered the hall, dressed in cloth of gold and silver, richly embroidered, and adorned with precious stones of great value. Here they found the king seated on a throne, and attended by all the principal nobles of his court. The embassadors advanced to pay their reverence to his majesty, bearing in their hands, in a richly-ornamented box, a letter from the Czar, with which they had been intrusted for him. There were a number of attendants also, who were loaded with rich and valuable presents which the embassadors had brought to offer to the king. The presents consisted of the most costly furs, tissues of gold and silver, precious stones, and the like, all productions of Russia, and of very great value.

The king received the embassadors in a very honorable manner, and made them an address of welcome in reply to the brief addresses of salutation and compliment which they first delivered to him. He received the letter from their hands and read it. The presents were deposited on tables which had been set for the purpose.

The letter stated that the Czar had sent the embassy to assure him of his desire "to improve the affection and good correspondence which had always existed, as well between his royal highness and himself as between their illustrious ancestors." It said also that "the same embassy being from thence to proceed to the court of Vienna, the Czar requested the king to help them on their journey." And finally it expressed the thanks of the Czar, for the "engineers and bombardiers" which the king had sent him during the past year, and who had been so useful to him in the siege of Azof.

The king, having read the letter, made a verbal reply to the embassadors, asking them to thank the Czar in his name for the friendly sentiments which his letter expressed, and for the splendid embassy which he had sent to him.

All this time the Czar himself, the author of the letter, was standing by, a quiet spectator of the scene, undistinguishable from the other secretaries and attendants that formed the embassadors' train.

After the ceremony of audience was completed the embassadors withdrew. They were reconducted to their lodgings with the same ceremonies as were observed in their coming out, and then spent the evening at a grand banquet provided for them by the elector. All the principal nobility of Prussia were present at this banquet, and after it was concluded the town was illuminated with a great display of fireworks, which continued until midnight.

The sending of a grand embassage like this from one royal or imperial potentate to another was a very common occurrence in those times. The pomp and parade with which they were accompanied were intended equally for the purpose of illustrating the magnificence of the government that sent them, and of offering a splendid token of respect to the one to which they were sent. Of course, the expense was enormous, both to the sovereign who sent and to the one who received the compliment. But such sovereigns as those were very willing to expend money in parades which exhibited before the world the evidences of their own grandeur and power, especially as the mass of the people, from whose toils the means of defraying the cost was ultimately to come, were so completely held in subjection by military power that they could not even complain, far less could they take any effectual measures for calling their oppressors to account. In governments that are organized at the present day, either by the establishment of new constitutions, or by the remodeling and reforming of old ones, all this is changed. The people understand now that all the money which is expended by their governments is ultimately paid by themselves, and they are gradually devising means by which they can themselves exercise a greater and greater control over these expenditures. They retain a far greater portion of the avails of their labor in their own hands, and expend it in adorning and making comfortable their own habitations, and cultivating the minds of their children, while they require the government officials to live, and travel, and transact their business in a more quiet and unpretending way than was customary of yore.

Thus, in traveling over most parts of the United States, you will find the people who cultivate the land living in comfortable, well-furnished houses, with separate rooms appropriately arranged for the different uses of the family. There is a carpet on the parlor floor, and there are books in the book-case, and good supplies of comfortable clothing in the closets. But then our embassadors and ministers in foreign courts are obliged to content themselves with what they consider very moderate salaries, which do not at all allow of their competing in style and splendor with the embassadors sent from the old despotic monarchies of Europe, under which the people who till the ground live in bare and wretched huts, and are supplied from year to year with only just enough of food and clothing to keep them alive and enable them to continue their toil.

But to return to Peter and his embassy. When the public reception was over Peter introduced himself privately to the king in his own name, and the king, in a quiet and unofficial manner, paid him great attention. There were to be many more public ceremonies, banquets, and parades for the embassy in the city during their stay, but Peter withdrew himself entirely from the scene, and went out to a certain bay, which extended about one hundred and fifty miles along the shore between Konigsberg and Dantzic, and occupied himself in examining the vessels which were there, and in sailing to and fro in them.

This bay you will find delineated on any map of Europe. It extends along the coast for a considerable distance between Konigsberg and Dantzic, on the southeastern shore of the Baltic Sea.

When the embassadors and their train had finished their banquetings and celebrations in Konigsberg, Peter joined them again, and the expedition proceeded to Dantzic. This was at that time, as it is now, a large commercial city, being one of the chief ports on the Baltic for the exportation of grain from Poland and other fertile countries in the interior.

By this time it began to be every where well known that Peter himself was traveling with the embassy. Peter would not, however, allow himself to be recognized at all, or permit any public notice to be taken of his presence, but went about freely in all the places that he visited with his own companions, just as if he were a private person, leaving all the public parades and receptions, and all the banquetings, and other state and civic ceremonies, to the three embassadors and their immediate train.

A great many elegant and expensive presents, however, were sent in to him, under pretense of sending them to the embassadors.

The expedition traveled on in this way along the coasts of the Baltic Sea, on the way toward Holland, which was the country that Peter was most eager to see. At every city where they stopped Peter went about examining the shipping. He was often attended by some important official person of the place, but in other respects he went without any ceremony whatever. He used to change his dress, putting on, in the different places that he visited, that which was worn by the common people of the town, so as not to attract any attention, and not even to be recognized as a foreigner. At one port, where there were a great many Dutch vessels that he wished to see, he wore the pea-jacket and the other sailor-like dress of a common Dutch skipper,[2] in order that he might ramble about at his ease along the docks, and mingle freely with the seafaring men, without attracting any notice at all.

The people of Holland were aware that the embassy was coming into their country, and that Peter himself accompanied it, and they accordingly prepared to receive the party with the highest marks of honor. As the embassy, after crossing the frontier, moved on toward Amsterdam, salutes were fired from the ramparts of all the great towns that they passed, the soldiers were drawn out, and civic processions, formed of magistrates and citizens, met them at the gates to conduct them through the streets. The windows, too, and the roofs of all the houses, were crowded with spectators.

Wherever they stopped at night bonfires and illuminations were made in honor of their arrival, and sometimes beautiful fireworks were played off in the evening before their palace windows.

Of course, there was a great desire felt every where among the spectators to discover which of the personages who followed in the train of the embassy was the Czar himself. They found it, however, impossible to determine this point, so completely had Peter disguised his person, and merged himself with the rest. Indeed, in some cases, when the procession was moving forward with great ceremony, the object of the closest scrutiny in every part for thousands of eyes, Peter himself was not in it at all. This was particularly the case on the occasion of the grand entry into Amsterdam. Peter left the party at a distance from the city, in order to go in quietly the next day, in company with some merchants with whom he had become acquainted. And, accordingly, while all Amsterdam had gathered into the streets, and were watching with the most intense curiosity every train as it passed, in order to discover which one contained the great Czar, the great Czar himself was several miles away, sitting quietly with his friends, the merchants, at a table in a common country inn.

The government and the people of Holland took a very great interest in this embassy, not only on account of the splendor of it, and the magnitude of the imperial power which it represented, but also on account of the business and pecuniary considerations which were involved. They wished very much to cultivate a good understanding with Russia, on account of the trade and commerce of that country, which was already very great, and was rapidly increasing. They determined, therefore, to show the embassy every mark of consideration and honor.

Jacob Abbott

Besides the measures which they adopted for giving the embassy itself a grand reception, the government set apart a spacious and splendid house in Amsterdam for the use of the Czar during his stay. They did this in a somewhat private and informal manner, it is true, for they knew that Peter did not wish that his presence with the embassy should be openly noticed in any way. They organized also a complete household for this palace, including servants, attendants, and officers of all kinds, in a style corresponding to the dignity of the exalted personage who was expected to occupy it.

But Peter, when he arrived, would not occupy the palace at all, but went into a quiet lodging among the shipping, where he could ramble about without constraint, and see all that was to be seen which could illustrate the art of navigation. The Dutch East India Company, which was then, perhaps, the greatest and most powerful association of merchants which had ever existed, had large ship-yards, where their vessels were built, at Saardam. Saardam was almost a suburb of Amsterdam, being situated on a deep river which empties into the Y, so called, which is the harbor of Amsterdam, and only a few miles from the town. Peter immediately made arrangements for going to these ship-yards and spending the time while the embassy remained in that part of the country in studying the construction of ships, and in becoming acquainted with the principal builders. Here, as the historians of the times say, he entered himself as a common ship-carpenter, being enrolled in the list of the company's workmen by the name Peter Michaelhoff, which was as nearly as possible his real name. He lived here several months, and devoted himself diligently to his work. He kept two or three of his companions with him—those whom he had brought from Moscow as his friends and associates on the tour; but they, it is said, did not take hold of the hard work with nearly as much zeal and energy as Peter displayed. Peter himself worked for the greatest part of every day among the other workmen, wearing also the same dress that they wore. When he was tired of work he would go out on the water, and sail and row about in the different sorts of boats, so as to make himself practically acquainted with the comparative effects of the various modes of construction.

The object which Peter had in view in all this was, doubtless, in a great measure, his own enjoyment for the time being. He was so much interested in the subject of ships and ship-building, and in every thing connected with navigation, that it was a delight to him to be in the midst of such scenes as were to be witnessed in the company's yards. He was still but a young man, and, like a great many other young men, he liked boats and the water. It is not probable, notwithstanding what is said by historians about his performances with the broad-axe, that he really did much serious work. Still he was naturally fond of mechanical occupations, as the fact of his making a wheelbarrow with which to construct a fortification, in his schoolboy days, sufficiently indicates.

Then, again, his being in the ship-yards so long, nominally as one of the workmen, gave him undoubtedly great facilities for observing every thing which it was important that he should know. Of course, he could not have seriously intended to make himself an actual and practical ship-carpenter, for, in the first place, the time was too short. A trade like that of a ship-carpenter requires years of apprenticeship to make a really good workman. Then, in the second place, the mechanical part of the work was not the part which it devolved upon him, as a sovereign intent on building up a navy for the protection of his empire, even to superintend. He could not, therefore, have seriously intended to learn to build ships himself, but only to make himself nominally a workman, partly for the pleasure which it gave him to place himself so wholly at home among the shipping, and partly for the sake of the increased opportunities which he thereby obtained of learning many things which it was important that he should know.

Travelers visiting Holland at the present day often go out to Saardam to see the little building that is still shown as the shop which Peter occupied while he was there. It is a small wooden building, leaning and bent with age and decrepitude and darkened by exposure and time. Within the last half century, however, in order to save so curious a relic from farther decay, the proprietors of the place have constructed around and over it an outer building of brick, which incloses the hut itself like a case. The sides of the outer building are formed of large, open arches, which allow the hut within to be seen. The ground on which the hut stands has also been laid out prettily as a garden, and is inclosed by a wall. Within this wall, and near the gate, is a very neat and pretty Dutch cottage, in which the custodian lives who shows the place to strangers.

While Peter was in the ship-yards the workmen knew who he was, but all persons were forbidden to gather around or gaze at him, or to interfere with him in any way by their notice or their attentions. They were to allow him to go and come as he pleased, without any molestation. These orders they obeyed as well as they could, as every one was desirous of treating their visitor in a manner as agreeable to him as possible, so as to prolong his stay.

Peter varied his amusements, while he thus resided in Saardam, by making occasional visits in a quiet and private way to certain friends in Amsterdam. He very seldom attended any of the great parades and celebrations which were continually taking place in honor of the embassy, but went only to the houses of men eminent in private life for their attainments in particular branches of knowledge, or for their experience or success as merchants or navigators. There was one person in particular that Peter became acquainted with in Amsterdam, whose company and conversation pleased him very much, and whom he frequently visited. This was a certain wealthy merchant, whose operations were on so vast a scale that he was accustomed to send off special expeditions at his own expense, all over the world, to explore new regions and discover new fields for his commercial enterprise. In order also to improve the accuracy of the methods employed by his ship-masters for ascertaining the latitude and longitude in navigating their ships, he built an observatory, and furnished it with the telescopes, quadrants, and other costly instruments necessary for making the observations—all at his own expense.

With this gentleman, and with the other persons in Amsterdam that Peter took a fancy to, he lived on very friendly and familiar terms. He often came in from Saardam to visit them, and would sometimes spend a considerable portion of the night in drinking and making merry with them. He assumed with these friends none of the reserve and dignity of demeanor that we should naturally associate with the idea of a king. Indeed, he was very blunt, and often rough and overbearing in his manners, not unfrequently doing and saying things which would scarcely be pardoned in a person of inferior station. When thwarted or opposed in any way he was irritable and violent, and he evinced continually a temper that was very far from being amiable. In a word, though his society was eagerly sought by all whom he was willing to associate with, he seems to have made no real friends. Those who knew him admired his intelligence and his energy, and they respected his power, but he was not a man that any one could love.

Amsterdam, though it was the great commercial centre of Holland—and, indeed, at that time, of the world—was not the capital of the country. The seat of government was then, as now, at the Hague. Accordingly, after remaining as long at Amsterdam as Peter wished to amuse himself in the ship-yards, the embassy moved on to the Hague, where it was received in a very formal and honorable manner by the king and the government. The presence of Peter could not be openly referred to, but very special and unusual honors were paid to the embassy in tacit recognition of it. At the Hague were resident ministers from all the great powers of Europe, and these all, with one exception, came to pay visits of ceremony to the embassadors, which visits were of course duly returned with great pomp and parade. The exception was the minister of France. There was a coolness existing at this time between the Russian and the French governments on account of something Peter had done in respect to the election of a king of Poland, which displeased the French king, and on this account the French minister declined taking part in the special honors paid to the embassy.

The Hague was at this time perhaps the most influential and powerful capital of Europe. It was the centre, in fact, of all important political movements and intrigues for the whole Continent. The embassy accordingly paused here, to take some rest from the fatigues and excitements of their long journey, and to allow Peter time to form and mature plans for future movements and operations.

[1] For the situation of Riga in relation to Moscow, and for that of the other places visited by the embassy, the reader must not fail to refer to a map of Europe.

[2] A skipper is the captain of a small vessel.

CHAPTER VII

CONCLUSION OF THE TOUR

1697

Peter compares the shipping of different nations—He determines to visit England—King William favors Peter's plans—Peter leaves Holland—Helvoetsluys—Arrival in England—His reception in London—The Duke of Leeds— Bishop Burnet—The bishop's opinion of Peter's character— Designs of Providence—Peter's curiosity—His conversations with the bishop—Peter takes a house "below bridge"—How he spent his time—Peter's dress—Curiosity in respect to him—His visit to the Tower—The various sights and shows of London—Workmen engaged—Peter's visit to Portsmouth and Spithead—Situation of Spithead—Appearance of the men-of-war—Grand naval spectacle—Present of a yacht— Peter sets sail—His treatment of his workmen—Wages retained—The engineer—Voyage to Holland—Peter rejoins the embassy—The Emperor Leopold—Interview with the Emperor of Germany—Feasts and festivities—Ceremonies —Bad tidings—Plans changed—Designs abandoned— Return to Moscow

While the embassy itself was occupied with the parades and ceremonies at the Hague, and at Utrecht, where they had a

Jacob Abbott

grand interview with the States-General, and at other great political centres, Peter traveled to and fro about Holland, visiting the different ports, and examining the shipping that he found in them, with the view of comparing the different models; for there were vessels in these ports from almost all the maritime countries of Europe. His attention was at last turned to some English ships, which pleased him very much. He liked the form of them better than that of the Dutch ships that he had seen. He soon made the acquaintance of a number of English ship-masters and ship-carpenters, and obtained from them, through an interpreter of course, a great deal of information in respect to the state of the art of ship-building in their country. He heard that in England naval carpentry had been reduced to a regular science, and that the forms and models of the vessels built there were determined by fixed mathematical principles, which every skillful and intelligent workman was expected to understand and to practice upon; whereas in Holland the carpenters worked by rote, each new set following their predecessors by a sort of mechanical imitation, without being governed by any principles or theory at all.

Peter immediately determined that he would go to England, and study the English methods himself on the spot, as he had already studied those of Holland.

The political relations between England and Holland were at this time of a very intimate character, the King of England being William, Prince of Orange.[1] The king, when he heard of Peter's intention, was much pleased, and determined to do all in his power to promote his views in making the journey. He immediately provided the Czar with a number of English attendants to accompany him on his voyage, and to remain with him in England during his stay. Among these were interpreters, secretaries, valets, and a number of cooks and other domestic servants. These persons were paid by the

King of England himself, and were ordered to accompany Peter to England, to remain with him all the time that he was there, and then to return with him to Holland, so that during the whole period of his absence he should have no trouble whatever in respect to his personal comforts or wants.

These preparations having been all made, the Czar left the embassy, and taking with him the company of servants which the king had provided, and also the few private friends who had been with him all the time since leaving Moscow, he sailed from a certain port in the south-western part of Holland, called Helvoetsluys, about the middle of the month of January.

He arrived without any accident at London. Here he at first took up his abode in a handsome house which the king had ordered to be provided and furnished for him. This house was in a genteel part of the town, where the noblemen and other persons belonging to the court resided. It was very pleasantly situated near the river, and the grounds pertaining to it extended down to the water side. Still it was far away from the part of the city which was devoted to commerce and the shipping, and Peter was not very well satisfied with it on that account. He, however, went to it at first, and continued to occupy it for some time.

In this house the Czar was visited by a great number of the nobility, and he visited them in return. He also received particular attentions from such members of the royal family as were then in London. But the person whose society pleased him most was one of the nobility, who, like himself, tools: a great interest in maritime affairs. This was the Duke of Leeds. The duke kept a number of boats at the foot of his gardens in London, and he and Peter used often to go out together in the river, and row and sail in them.

Jacob Abbott

Among other attentions which were paid to Peter by the government during his stay in London, one was the appointment of a person to attend upon him for the purpose of giving him, at any time, such explanations or such information as he might desire in respect to the various institutions of England, whether those relating to government, to education, or to religion. The person thus appointed was Bishop Burnet, a very distinguished dignitary of the Church. The bishop could, of course, only converse with Peter through interpreters, but the practice of conversing in that way was very common in those days, and persons were specially trained and educated to translate the language of one person to another in an easy and agreeable manner. In this way Bishop Burnet held from time to time various interviews with the Czar, but it seems that he did not form a very favorable opinion of his temper and character. The bishop, in an account of these interviews which he subsequently wrote, said that Peter was a man of strong capacity, and of much better general education than might have been expected from the manner of life which he had led, but that he was of a very hot and violent temper, and that he was very brutal in his language and demeanor when he was in a passion. The bishop expressed himself quite strongly on this point, saying that he could not but adore the depth of the providence of God that had raised such a furious man to so absolute an authority over so great a part of the world.

It was seen in the end how wise was the arrangement of Providence in the selection of this instrument for the accomplishment of its designs—for the reforms which, notwithstanding the violence of his personal character, and the unjust and cruel deeds which he sometimes performed, Peter was the means of introducing, and those to which the changes that he made afterward led, have advanced, and are still advancing more and more every year, the whole moral, political, and social condition of all the populations of Northern Europe and Asia, and have instituted a course of progress and improvement which will, perhaps, go on, without being again arrested, to the end of time.

The bishop says that he found Peter somewhat curious to learn what the political and religious institutions of England were, but that he did not manifest any intention or desire to introduce them into his own country. The chief topic which interested him, even in talking with the bishop, was that of his purposes and plans in respect to ships and shipping. He gave the bishop an account of what he had done, and of what he intended to do, for the elevation and improvement of his people; but all his plans of this kind were confined to such improvements as would tend to the extension and aggrandizement of his own power. In other words, the ultimate object of the reforms which he was desirous of introducing was not the comfort and happiness of the people themselves, but his own exaltation and glory among the potentates of the earth as their hereditary and despotic sovereign.

After remaining some time in the residence which the king had provided for him at the court end of the town, Peter contrived to have a house set apart for him "below bridge," as the phrase was—that is, among the shipping. There was but one bridge across the Thames in those days, and the position of that one, of course, determined the limit of that part of the river and town that could be devoted to the purposes of commerce and navigation, for ships, of course, could not go above it. The house which was now provided for Peter was near the royal ship-yard. There was a back gate which opened from the yard of the house into the ship-yard, so that Peter could go and come when he pleased. Peter remained in this new lodging for some time. He often went into the ship-yard to watch the men at their operations, and while there would often take up the tools and work with them. At other times he would ramble about the streets of

Jacob Abbott

London in company with his two or three particular friends, examining every thing which was new or strange to him, and talking with his companions in respect to the expediency or feasibility of introducing the article or the usage, whatever it might be, as an improvement, into his own dominions.

In these excursions Peter was sometimes dressed in the English citizen's dress, and sometimes he wore the dress of a common sailor. In the latter costume he found that he could walk about more freely on the wharves and along the docks without attracting observation, but, notwithstanding all that he could do to disguise himself, he was often discovered. Some person, perhaps, who had seen him and his friends in the ship-yard, would recognize him and point him out. Then it would be whispered from one to another among the by-standers that that was the Russian Emperor, and people would follow him where he went, or gather around him where he was standing. In such cases as this, as soon as Peter found that he was recognized, and was beginning to attract attention, he always went immediately away.

Among other objects of interest which attracted Peter's attention in London was the Tower, where there was kept then, as now, an immense collection of arms of all kinds. This collection consists not only of a vast store of the weapons in use at the present day, laid up there to be ready for service whenever they may be required, but also a great number and variety of specimens of those which were employed in former ages, but are now superseded by new inventions. Peter, as might naturally have been expected, took a great deal of interest in examining these collections.

In respect to all the more ordinary objects of interest for strangers in London, the shops, the theatres, the parks, the gay parties given by the nobility at the West End, and other such spectacles, Peter saw them all, but he paid very little attention to them. His thoughts were almost entirely engrossed by subjects connected with his navy. He found, as he had expected from what he heard in Holland, that the English ship-carpenters had reduced their business quite to a system, being accustomed to determine the proportions of the model by fixed principles, and to work, in the construction of the ship, from drafts made by rule. When he was in the ship-yard he studied this subject very attentively; and although it was, of course, impossible that in so short a time he should make himself fully master of it, he was still able to obtain such a general insight into the nature of the method as would very much assist him in making arrangements for introducing it into his own country.

There was another measure which he took that was even more important still. He availed himself of every opportunity which was afforded him, while engaged in the ship-yards and docks, to become acquainted with the workmen, especially the head workmen of the yards, and he engaged a number of them to go to Russia, and enter into his service there in the work of building his navy.

In a word, the Czar was much better pleased with the manner in which the work of ship-building was carried on in England than with any thing that he had seen in Holland; so much so that he said he wished that he had come directly to England at first, inasmuch as now, since he had seen how much superior were the English methods, he considered the long stay which he had made in Holland as pretty nearly lost time.

After remaining as long and learning as much in the dock-yards in and below London as he thought the time at his command would allow, Peter went to Portsmouth to visit the royal navy at anchor there. The arrangement which nature has made of the southern coast of England seems almost as if

Jacob Abbott

expressly intended for the accommodation of a great national and mercantile marine. In the first place, at the town of Portsmouth, there is a deep and spacious harbor entirely surrounded and protected by land. Then at a few miles distant, off the coast, lies the Isle of Wight, which brings under shelter a sheet of water not less than five miles wide and twenty miles long, where all the fleets and navies of the world might lie at anchor in safety. There is an open access to this sound both from the east and from the west, and yet the shores curve in such a manner that both entrances are well protected from the ingress of storms.

Directly opposite to Portsmouth, and within this inclosed sea, is a place where the water is just of the right depth, and the bottom of just the right conformation for the convenient anchoring of ships of war. This place is called Spithead, and it forms one of the most famous anchoring grounds in the world. It is here that the vast fleets of the English navy assemble, and here the ships come to anchor, when returning home from their distant voyages. The view of these grim-looking sea-monsters, with their double and triple rows of guns, lying quietly at their moorings, as seen by the spectator from the deck of the steamer which glides through and among them, on the way from Portsmouth to the Isle of Wight, is extremely imposing. Indeed, when considered by a mind capable of understanding in some degree the vast magnitude and extension of the power which lies thus reposing there, the spectacle becomes truly sublime.

In order to give Peter a favorable opportunity to see the fleet at Spithead, the King of England commissioned the admiral in command of the navy to accompany him to Portsmouth, and to put the fleet to sea, with the view of exhibiting a mock naval engagement in the Channel. Nothing could exceed the pleasure which this spectacle afforded to the Czar. He expressed his admiration of it in the most glowing terms, and said that he verily believed that an admiral of the English fleet was a happier man than the Czar of Muscovy.

At length, when the time arrived for Peter to set out on his return to his own dominions, the King of England made him a present of a beautiful yacht, which had been built for his own use in his voyages between England and Holland. The name of the yacht was the Royal Transport. It was an armed vessel, carrying twenty-four guns, and was well-built, and richly finished and furnished in every respect. The Czar set sail from England in this yacht, taking with him the companions that he had brought with him into England, and also a considerable number of the persons whom he had engaged to enter into his service in Russia. Some of these persons were to be employed in the building of ships, and others in the construction of a canal to connect the River Don with the River Wolga. The Don flows into the Black and the Wolga into the Caspian Sea, and the object of the canal was to allow Peter's vessels to pass from one sea into the other at pleasure. As soon as the canal should be opened, ships could be built on either river for use in either sea.

The persons who had been engaged for these various purposes were promised, of course, very large rewards to induce them to leave their country. Many of them afterward had occasion bitterly to regret their having entered the service of such a master. They complained that, after their arrival in Russia, Peter treated them in a very unjust and arbitrary manner. They were held as prisoners more than as salaried workmen, being very closely watched and guarded to prevent their making their escape and going back to their own country before finishing what Peter wished them to do. Then, a large portion of their pay was kept back, on the plea that it was necessary for the emperor to have security in his own hands for their fidelity in the performance of their work, and for their remaining at their posts until their work was

Jacob Abbott

done. There was one gentleman in particular, a Scotch mathematician and engineer, who had been educated at the University of Aberdeen, that complained of the treatment which he received in a full and formal protest, which he addressed to Peter in writing, and which is still on record. He makes out a very strong case in respect to the injustice with which he was treated.

But, however disappointed these gentlemen may have been in the end, they left England in the emperor's beautiful yacht, much elated with the honor they had received in being selected by such a potentate for the execution of important trusts in a distant land, and with high anticipations of the fame and fortune which they expected to acquire before the time should arrive for them to return to their own country. From England the yacht sailed to Holland, where Peter disembarked, in order to join the embassy and accompany them in their visits to some other courts in Central Europe before returning home.

He first went to Vienna. He still nominally preserved his incognito; but the Emperor Leopold, who was at that time the Emperor of Germany, gave him a very peculiar sort of reception. He came out to the door of his antechamber to meet Peter at the head of a certain back staircase communicating with the apartment, which was intended for his own private use. Peter was accompanied by General Le Fort, the chief embassador, at this interview, and he was conducted up the staircase by two grand officers of the Austrian court—the grand chamberlain and the grand equerry. After the two potentates had been introduced to each other, the emperor, who had taken off his hat to bow to the Czar, put it on again, but Peter remained uncovered, on the ground that he was not at that time acting in his own character as Czar. The emperor, seeing this, took off his hat again, and both remained uncovered during the interview.

After this a great many parades and celebrations took place in Vienna, all ostensibly in honor of the embassy, but really and truly in honor of Peter himself, who still preserved his incognito. At many of these festivities Peter attended, taking his place with the rest of the subordinates in the train of the embassy, but he never appeared in his own true character. Still he was known, and he was the object of a great many indirect but very marked attentions. On one occasion, for example, there was a masked ball in the palace of the emperor; Peter appeared there dressed as a peasant of West Friesland, which is a part of North Holland, where the costumes worn by the common people were then, as indeed they are at the present day, very marked and peculiar. The Emperor of Germany appeared also at this ball in a feigned character—that of a host at an entertainment, and he had thirty-two pages in attendance upon him, all dressed as butlers. In the course of the evening one of the pages brought out to the emperor a very curious and costly glass, which he filled with wine and presented to the emperor, who then approached Peter and drank to the health of the peasant of West Friesland, saying at the same time, with a meaning look, that he was well aware of the inviolable affection which the peasant felt for the Czar of Muscovy. Peter, in return, drank to the health of the host, saying he was aware of the inviolable affection he felt for the Emperor of Germany.

These toasts were received by the whole company with great applause, and after they were drunk the emperor gave Peter the curious glass from which he had drunk, desiring him to keep it as a souvenir of the occasion.

These festivities in honor of the embassy at Vienna were at length suddenly interrupted by the arrival of tidings from Moscow that a rebellion had broken out there against Peter's government. This intelligence changed at once all Peter's plans. He had intended to go to Venice and to Rome, but he now at once abandoned these designs, and setting out abruptly from Vienna, with General Le Fort, and a train of about thirty persons, he traveled with the utmost possible dispatch to Moscow.

[1] William, Prince of Orange, was descended on the female side from the English royal family, and was a Protestant. Accordingly, when James II., and with him the Catholic branch of the royal family of England, was expelled from the throne, the British Parliament called upon William to ascend it, he being the next heir on the Protestant side.

CHAPTER VIII

THE REBELLION

1698

Precautions taken by the Czar—His uneasiness—His fury against his enemies—His revolting appearance—Imperfect communication—Conspiracy—Arguments used—Details of the plot—Pretext of the guards—They commence their march—Alarm in Moscow—General Gordon—A parley with the rebels—Influence of the Church—The clergy on the side of the rebels—Conservatism—The Russian clergy—The armies prepare for battle—The insurgents defeated—Massacre of prisoners—Confession—Peter's arrival at Moscow—His terrible severity—Peter becomes himself an executioner—The Guards—Gibbets—The writer of the address to Sophia—The old Russian nobility—Arrival of artisans—Retirement of Sophia—Her death

It will be recollected by the reader that Peter, before he set out on his tour, took every possible precaution to guard against the danger of disturbances in his dominions during his absence. The Princess Sophia was closely confined in her convent. All that portion of the old Russian Guards that he thought most likely to be dissatisfied with his proposed reforms, and to take part with Sophia, he removed to fortresses at a great distance from Moscow. Moscow itself was garrisoned with troops selected expressly with reference to their supposed fidelity to his interests, and the men who were to command them, as well as the great civil officers to whom the administration of the government was committed during his absence, were appointed on the same principle.

But, notwithstanding all these precautions, Peter did not feel entirely safe. He was well aware of Sophia's ambition, and of her skill in intrigue, and during the whole progress of his tour he anxiously watched the tidings which he received from Moscow, ready to return at a moment's warning in case of necessity. He often spoke on this subject to those with whom he was on terms of familiar intercourse. On such occasions he would get into a great rage in denouncing his enemies, and in threatening vengeance against them in case they made any movement to resist his authority while he was away. At such times he would utter most dreadful imprecations against those who should dare to oppose him, and would work himself up into such a fury as to give those who conversed with him an exceedingly unfavorable opinion of his temper and character. The ugly aspect which his countenance and demeanor exhibited at such times was greatly aggravated by a nervous affection of the head and face which attacked him, particularly when he was in a passion, and which produced convulsive twitches of the muscles that drew his head by jerks to one side, and distorted his face in a manner that was dreadful to behold. It was said that this disorder was first induced in his childhood by some one of the terrible frights through which he passed. However this may have been, the affection seemed to increase as he grew older, and as the attacks of it were most decided and violent when he was in a passion, they had the effect, in connection with his coarse and dreadful language and violent demeanor, to make him appear at such times more like some ugly monster of fiction than like a man.

The result, in respect to the conduct of his enemies during his absence, was what he feared. After he had been gone away for some months they began to conspire against him. The means of communication between different countries were quite imperfect in those days, so that very little exact information came back to Russia in respect to the emperor's movements. The nobles who were opposed to him began to represent to the people that he had gone nobody knew where, and that it was wholly uncertain whether he would ever return. Besides, if he did return, they said it would only be to bring with him a fresh importation of foreign favorites and foreign manners, and to proceed more vigorously than ever in his work of superseding and subverting all the good old customs of the land, and displacing the ancient native families from all places of consideration and honor, in order to make room for the swarms of miserable foreign adventurers that he would bring home with him in his train.

By these and similar representations the opposition so far increased and strengthened their party that, at length, they matured their arrangements for an open outbreak. Their plan was, first, to take possession of the city by means of the Guards, who were to be recalled for this purpose from their distant posts, and by their assistance to murder all the foreigners. They were then to issue a proclamation declaring that Peter, by leaving the country and remaining so long away, had virtually abdicated the government; and also a formal address to the Princess Sophia, calling upon her to ascend the throne in his stead.

In executing this plan, negotiations were first cautiously opened with the Guards, and they readily acceded to the proposals made to them. A committee of three persons was appointed to draw up the address to Sophia, and the precise details of the movements which were to take place on the arrival of the Guards at the gates of Moscow were all

Jacob Abbott

arranged. The Guards, of course, required some pretext for leaving their posts and coming toward the city, independent of the real cause, for the conspirators within the city were not prepared to rise and declare the throne vacant until the Guards had actually arrived. Accordingly, while the conspirators remained quiet, the Guards began to complain of various grievances under which they suffered, particularly that they were not paid their wages regularly, and they declared their determination to march to Moscow and obtain redress. The government—that is, the regency that Peter had left in charge—sent out deputies, who attempted to pacify them, but could not succeed. The Guards insisted that they would go with their complaints to Moscow. They commenced their march. The number of men was about ten thousand. They pretended that they were only going to the city to represent their case themselves directly to the government, and then to march back again in a peaceable manner. They wished to know, too, they said, what had become of the Czar. They could not depend upon the rumors which came to them at so great a distance, and they were determined to inform themselves on the spot whether he were alive or dead, and when he was coming home.

The deputies returned with all speed to Moscow, and reported that the Guards were on their march in full strength toward the city. The whole city was thrown into a state of consternation. Many of the leading families, anticipating serious trouble, moved away. Others packed up and concealed their valuables. The government, too, though not yet suspecting the real design of the Guards in the movement which they were making, were greatly alarmed. They immediately ordered a large armed force to go and meet the insurgents. This force was commanded by General Gordon, the officer whom Peter had made general-in-chief of the army before he set out on his tour.

General Gordon came up with the rebels about forty miles from Moscow. As soon as he came near to them he halted, and sent forward a deputation from his camp to confer with the leaders, in the hope of coming to some amicable settlement of the difficulty. This deputation consisted of Russian nobles of ancient and established rank and consideration in the country, who had volunteered to accompany the general in his expedition. General Gordon himself was one of the hated foreigners, and of course his appearance, if he had gone himself to negotiate with the rebels, would have perhaps only exasperated and inflamed them more than ever.

The deputation held a conference with the leaders of the Guards, and made them very conciliatory offers. They promised that if they would return to their duty the government would not only overlook the serious offense which they had committed in leaving their posts and marching upon Moscow, but would inquire into and redress all their grievances. But the Guards refused to be satisfied. They were determined, they said, to march to Moscow. They wished to ascertain for themselves whether Peter was dead or alive, and if alive, what had become of him. They therefore were going on, and, if General Gordon and his troops attempted to oppose them, they would fight it out and see which was the strongest.

In civil commotions of this kind occurring in any of the ancient non-Protestant countries in Europe, it is always a question of the utmost moment which side the Church and the clergy espouse. It is true that the Church and the clergy do not fight themselves, and so do not add any thing to the physical strength of the party which they befriend, but they add enormously to its moral strength, that is, to its confidence and courage. Men have a sort of instinctive respect and fear for constituted authorities of any kind, and, though often willing to plot against them, are still very apt to

Jacob Abbott

falter and fall back when the time comes for the actual collision. The feeling that, after all, they are in the wrong in fighting against the government of their country, weakens them extremely, and makes them ready to abandon the struggle in panic and dismay on the first unfavorable turn of fortune. But if they have the Church and the clergy on their side, this state of things is quite changed. The sanction of religion—the thought that they are fighting in the cause of God and of duty, nerves their arms, and gives them that confidence in the result which is almost essential to victory.

It was so in this case. There was no class in the community more opposed to the Czar's proposed improvements and reforms than the Church. Indeed, it is always so. The Church and the clergy are always found in these countries on the side of opposition to progress and improvement. It is not that they are really opposed to improvement itself for its own sake, but that they are so afraid of change. They call themselves Conservatives, and wish to preserve every thing as it is. They hate the process of pulling down. Now, if a thing is good, it is better, of course, to preserve it; but, on the other hand, if it is bad, it is better that it should be pulled down. When, therefore, you are asked whether you are a Conservative or not, reply that that depends upon the character of the institution or the usage which is attacked. If it is good, let it stand. If it is bad, let it be destroyed.

In the case of Peter's proposed improvements and reforms the Church and the clergy were Conservatives of the most determined character. Of course, the plotters of the conspiracy in Moscow were in communication with the patriarch and the leading ecclesiastics in forming their plans; and in arranging for the marching of the Guards to the capital they took care to have priests with them to encourage them in the movement, and to assure them that in opposing the present government and restoring Sophia to power they were serving the cause of God and religion by promoting the expulsion from the country of the infidel foreigners that were coming in in such numbers, and subverting all the good old usages and customs of the realm.

It was this sympathy on the part of the clergy which gave the officers and soldiers of the Guards their courage and confidence in daring to persist in their march to Moscow in defiance of the army of General Gordon, brought out to oppose them.

The two armies approached each other. General Gordon, as is usual in such cases, ordered a battery of artillery which he had brought up in the road before the Guards to fire, but he directed that the guns should be pointed so high that the balls should go over the heads of the enemy. His object was to intimidate them. But the effect was the contrary. The priests, who had come into the army of the insurgents to encourage them in the fight, told them that a miracle had been performed. God had averted the balls from them, they said. They were fighting for the honor of his cause and for the defense of his holy religion, and they might rely upon it that he would not suffer them to be harmed.

But these assurances of the priests proved, unfortunately for the poor Guards, to be entirely unfounded. When General Gordon found that firing over the heads of the rebels did no good, ho gave up at once all hope of any adjustment of the difficulty, and he determined to restrain himself no longer, but to put forth the whole of his strength, and kill and destroy all before him in the most determined and merciless manner. A furious battle followed, in which the Guards were entirely defeated. Two or three thousand of them were killed, and all the rest were surrounded and made prisoners.

The first step taken by General Gordon, with the advice of

the Russian nobles who had accompanied him, was to count off the prisoners and hang every tenth man. The next was to put the officers to the torture, in order to compel them to confess what their real object was in marching to Moscow. After enduring their tortures as long as human nature could bear them, they confessed that the movement was a concerted one, made in connection with a conspiracy within the city, and that the object was to subvert the present government, and to liberate the Princess Sophia and place her upon the throne. They also gave the names of a number of prominent persons in Moscow who, they said, were the leaders of the conspiracy.

It was in this state of the affair that the tidings of what had occurred reached Peter in Vienna, as is related in the last chapter. He immediately set out on his return to Moscow in a state of rage and fury against the rebels that it would be impossible to describe. As he arrived at the capital, he commenced an inquisition into the affair by putting every body to the torture whom he supposed to be implicated as a leader in it. From the agony of these sufferers he extorted the names of innumerable victims, who, as fast as they were named, were seized and put to death. There were a great many of the ancient nobles thus condemned, a great many ladies of high rank, and large numbers of priests. These persons were all executed, or rather massacred, in the most reckless and merciless manner. Some were beheaded; some were broken on the wheel, and then left to die in horrible agonies. Many were buried alive, their heads only being left above the ground. It is said that Peter took such a savage delight in these punishments, that he executed many of the victims with his own hands. At one time, when half intoxicated at a banquet, he ordered twenty of his prisoners to be brought in, and then, with his brandy before him, which was his favorite drink, and which he often drank to excess, he caused them to be led, one after another, to the block, that he might cut off their heads himself. He took a drink of brandy after each execution while the officers were bringing forward the next man. He was just an hour, it was said, in cutting off the twenty heads, which allows of an average of three minutes to each man. This story is almost too horrible to be believed, but, unfortunately, it comports too well with the general character which Peter has always sustained in the opinion of mankind in respect to the desperate and reckless cruelty to which he could be aroused under the influence of intoxication and anger.

About two thousand of the Guards were beheaded. The bodies of these men were laid upon the ground in a public place, arranged in rows, with their heads lying beside them. They covered more than an acre of ground. Here they were allowed to lie all the remainder of the winter, as long, in fact, as the flesh continued frozen, and then, when the spring came on, they were thrown together into a deep ditch, dug to receive them, and thus were buried.

There were also a great number of gibbets set up on all the roads leading to Moscow, and upon these gibbets men were hung, and the bodies allowed to remain there, like the beheaded Guards upon the ground, until the spring.

As for the Princess Sophia, she was still in the convent where Peter had placed her, the conspirators not having reached the point of liberating her before their plot was discovered. Peter, however, caused the three authors of the address, which was to have been made to Sophia, calling upon her to assume the crown, to be sent to the convent, and there hung before Sophia's windows. And then, by his orders, the arm of the principal man among them was cut off, the address was put into his hand, and, when the fingers had stiffened around it, the limb was fixed to the wall in Sophia's chamber, as if in the act of offering her the address, and ordered to remain so until the address should drop, of itself, upon the floor.

Such were the horrible means by which Peter attempted to strike terror into his subjects, and to put down the spirit of conspiracy and rebellion. He doubtless thought that it was only by such severities as these that the end could be effectually attained. At all events, the end was attained. The rebellion was completely suppressed, and all open opposition to the progress of the Czar's proposed improvements and reforms ceased. The few leading nobles who adhered to the old customs and usages of the realm retired from all connection with public affairs, and lived thenceforth in seclusion, mourning, like good Conservatives, the triumph of the spirit of radicalism and innovation which was leading the country, as they thought, to certain ruin. The old Guards, whom it had been proved so utterly impossible to bring over to Peter's views, were disbanded, and other troops, organized on a different system, were embodied in their stead. By this time the English ship-builders, and the other mechanics and artisans that Peter had engaged, began to arrive in the country, and the way was open for the emperor to go on vigorously in the accomplishment of his favorite and long-cherished plans.

The Princess Sophia, worn out with the agitations and dangers through which she had passed, and crushed in spirit by the dreadful scenes to which her brother had exposed her, now determined to withdraw wholly from the scene. She took the veil in the convent where she was confined, and went as a nun into the cloisters with the other sisters. The name that she assumed was Marpha.

Of course, all her ambitious aspirations were now forever extinguished, and the last gleam of earthly hope faded away from her mind. She pined away under the influences of disappointment, hopeless vexation, and bitter grief for about six years, and then the nuns of the convent followed the body of sister Marpha to the tomb.

Jacob Abbott

CHAPTER IX

REFORMS

1700-1701

Peter begins his proposed reforms—Remodeling the army—
Changes of dress—The officers—New appointments—
Motives and object of the Czar—Means of revenue—
Mysterious power—The secret of it—Management of a
standing army—Artful contrivances—Despotism *versus*
freedom—Policy of the American people—Standing armies—
The American government is weak—The people reserve their
strength—Peter's policy—The Church—Conservatism of the
clergy—The patriarch—Ancient custom—The emperor on the
procession—Emblems—Peter's reflections on the subject—
Peter's determination—He proceeds cautiously—Contest with
the bishops—Peter is victorious—Other reforms—Collection
of the revenues—New revenue system—Manners and
customs of the people—Mustaches and beards—The long
dresses suppressed—Effect of ridicule—The jester's marriage
—Curious sleeves—Mode of manoeuvring the sleeve—The
boyars in the streets—Long trains of attendants—Peter
changes the whole system—Motives of the Czar—Ultimate
effect of his reforms

As soon as Peter had sufficiently glutted his vengeance on

those whom he chose to consider, whether justly or unjustly, as implicated in the rebellion, he turned his attention at once to the work of introducing the improvements and reforms which had been suggested to him by what he had seen in the western countries of Europe. There was a great deal of secret hostility to the changes which he thus wished to make, although every thing like open opposition to his will had been effectually put down by the terrible severity of his dealings with the rebels. He continued to urge his plans of reform during the whole course of his reign, and though he met from time to time with a great variety of difficulties in his efforts to carry them into effect, he was in the end triumphantly successful in establishing and maintaining them. I shall proceed to give a general account of these reforms in this chapter, notwithstanding that the work of introducing them extended over a period of many years subsequent to this time.

The first thing to which the Czar gave his attention was the complete remodeling of his army. He established new regiments in place of the old Guards, and put his whole army on a new footing. He abolished the dress which the Guards had been accustomed to wear—an ancient Muscovite costume, which, like the dress of the Highlanders of Scotland, was strongly associated in the minds of the men with ancient national customs, many of which the emperor now wished to abolish. Instead of this old costume the emperor dressed his new troops in a modern military uniform. This was not only much more convenient than the old dress, but the change exerted a great influence in disenthralling the minds of the men from the influence of old ideas and associations. It made them feel at once as if they were new men, belonging to a new age—one marked by a new and higher civilization than they had been accustomed to in former years. The effect which was produced by this simple change was very marked—so great is the influence of dress and other outward symbols on the sentiments of the mind and on the character.

Peter had made a somewhat similar change to this, in the case of his household troops and private body-guard, at the suggestion of General Le Fort, some time previous to this period, but now he carried the same reform into effect in respect to his whole army.

In addition to these improvements in the dress and discipline of the men, Peter adopted an entirely new system in officering his troops. A great many of the old officers—all those who were proved or even suspected of being hostile to him and to his measures—had been beheaded or sent into banishment, and others still had been dismissed from the service. Peter filled all these vacant posts by bringing forward and appointing the sons of the nobility, making his selections from those families who were either already inclined to his side, or who he supposed might be brought over by the influence of appointments and honors conferred upon their sons.

Of course, the great object of the Czar in thus reorganizing his army and increasing the military strength of the empire was not the more effectual protection of the country from foreign enemies, or from any domestic violence which might threaten to disturb the peace or endanger the property of the public, but only the confirming and perpetuating his own power as the sovereign ruler of it. It is true that such potentates as Peter really desire that the countries over which they rule should prosper, and should increase in wealth and population; but then they do this usually only as the proprietor of an estate might wish to improve his property, that is, simply with an eye to his own interest as the owner of it. In reforming his army, and placing it, as he did, on a new and far more efficient footing than before, Peter's main inducement was to increase and secure his own power. He wished also, doubtless, to preserve the peace of the country, in order that the inhabitants might go on regularly in the pursuit of their industrial occupations, for their ability to pay the taxes required for the large revenues which he wished to raise would increase or diminish, he knew very well, just in proportion to the productiveness of the general industry; still, his own exaltation and grandeur were the ultimate objects in view.

Young persons, when they read in history of the power which many great tyrants have exercised, and the atrocious crimes which they have committed against the rights of their fellow-men, sometimes wonder how it is that one man can acquire or retain so absolute a dominion over so many millions as to induce them to kill each other in such vast numbers at his bidding; for, of course, it is but a very small number of the victims of a tyrant's injustice or cruelty that are executed by his own hand. How is it, then, that one weak and often despicable and hateful man can acquire and retain such an ascendency over those that stand around him, that they shall all be ready to draw their swords instantaneously at his bidding, and seize and destroy, without hesitation and without mercy, whomsoever he may choose to designate as the object of his rage and vengeance? How is it that the wealthiest, the most respected, and the most popular citizens of the state, though surrounded with servants and with multitudes of friends, have no power to resist when one of these Neros conceives the idea of striking him down, but must yield without a struggle to his fate, as if to inevitable destiny?

The secret of this extraordinary submission of millions to one is always an army. The tyrant, under the pretense of providing the means for the proper execution of just and righteous laws, and the maintenance of peace and order in the community, organizes an army. He contrives so to arrange and regulate this force as to separate it completely from the rest of the community, so as to extinguish as far as possible all the sympathies which might otherwise exist between the soldiers and the citizens. Marriage is discouraged, so that the troops may not be bound to the community by any family ties. The regiments arc quartered in barracks built and appropriated to their especial use, and they are continually changed from one set of barracks to another, in order to prevent their forming too intimate an acquaintance with any portion of the community, or learning to feel any common interest or sympathy with them. Then, as a reward for their privations, the soldiers are allowed, with very little remonstrance or restraint, to indulge freely in all such habits of dissipation and vice as will not at once interfere with military discipline, or deteriorate from the efficiency of the whole body as a military corps. The soldiers soon learn to love the idle and dissolute lives which they are allowed to lead. The officers, especially those in the higher grades of rank, are paid large salaries, are clothed in a gaudy dress which is adorned with many decorations, and they are treated every where with great consideration. Thus they become devoted to the will of the government, and lose gradually all regard for, and all sympathy with the rights and welfare of the people. There is a tacit agreement between them and the government, by which they are bound to keep the people in a state of utter and abject submission to the despot's will, while he, on his part, is bound to collect from the people thus subdued the sums of money necessary for their pay. Thus it is the standing army which is that great and terrible sword by means of which one man is able to strike awe into the hearts of so many millions, and hold them all so entirely subject to his will.

It is in consequence of having observed the effect of such armaments in the despotisms of Europe and Asia that the free governments of modern times take good care not to allow large standing armies to be formed. Instead of this the people organize themselves into armed bands, in connection with which they meet and practice military evolutions on appointed days, and then separate and go back to their wives and to their children, and to their usual occupations, while in the despotic countries where large standing armies are maintained, the people are strictly forbidden to possess arms, or to form organizations, or to take measures of any kind that could tend to increase their means of defense against their oppressors in the event of a struggle.

The consequence is, that under the free governments of the present day the people are strong and the government is weak. The standing army of France consists at the present time[1] of five hundred thousand men, completely armed and equipped, and devoted all the time to the study and practice of the art of war. By means of this force one man is able to keep the whole population of the country in a state of complete and unquestioning submission to his will. In the United States, on the other hand, with a population nearly as great, the standing army seldom amounts to an effective force of fifteen thousand men; and if a president of the United States were to attempt by means of it to prolong his term of office, or to accomplish any other violent end, there is, perhaps, not a single state in the Union, the population of which would not alone be able to put him down—so strong are the people with us, and so weak, in opposition to them, the government and the army.

It is often made a subject of reproach by European writers and speakers, in commenting on the state of things in America, that the government is so weak; but this we consider not our reproach, but our glory. The government is indeed weak. The people take good care to keep it weak. But the nation is not weak; the nation is strong. The difference is,

Jacob Abbott

that in our country the nation chooses to retain its power in its own hands. The people make the government strong enough from time to time for all the purposes which they wish it to accomplish. When occasion shall arise, the strength thus to be imparted to it may be increased almost indefinitely, according to the nature of the emergency. In the mean time, the people consider themselves the safest depositary of their reserved power.

But to return to Peter. Of course, his policy was the reverse of ours. He wished to make his army as efficient as possible, and to cut it off as completely as possible from all communion and sympathy with the people, so as to keep it in close and absolute subjection to his own individual will. The measures which he adopted were admirably adapted to this purpose. By means of them he greatly strengthened his power, and established it on a firm and permanent basis.

Peter did not forget that, during the late rebellion, the influence of the Church and that of all the leading ecclesiastics had been against him. This was necessarily the case; for, in a Church constituted as that of Russia then was, the powers and prerogatives of the priests rested, not on reason or right, but on ancient customs. The priests would therefore naturally be opposed to all changes—even improvements—in the usages and institutions of the realm, for fear that the system of reform, if once entered upon, might extend to and interfere with their ancient prerogatives and privileges. An established Church in any country, where, by means of the establishment, the priests or the ministers hold positions which secure to them the possession of wealth or power, is always opposed to every species of change. It hates even the very name of reform.

Peter determined to bring the Russian Church more under his own control. Up to that time it had been, in a great measure, independent. The head of it was an ecclesiastic of great power and dignity, called the Patriarch. The jurisdiction of this patriarch extended over all the eastern portion of the Christian world, and his position and power were very similar to those of the Pope of Rome, who reigned over the whole western portion.

Indeed, so exalted was the position and dignity of the patriarch, and so great was the veneration in which he was held by the people, that he was, as it were, the spiritual sovereign of the country, just as Peter was the civil and military sovereign; and on certain great religious ceremonies he even took precedence of the Czar himself, and actually received homage from him. At one of the great religious anniversaries, which was always celebrated with great pomp and parade, it was customary for the patriarch to ride through the street on horseback, with the Czar walking before him holding the bridle of the horse. The bridle used, on these occasions was very long, like a pair of reins, and was made of the richest material, and ornamented with golden embroidery. The Czar walked on in advance, with the loop of the bridle lying over his arm. Then came three or four great nobles of the court, who held up the reins behind the Czar, one of them taking hold close to the horse's head, so as to guide and control the movements of the animal. The patriarch, who, as is the custom with priests, was dressed in long robes, which prevented his mounting the horse in the usual manner, sat upon a square flat seat which was placed upon the horse's back by way of saddle, and rode in that manner, with his feet hanging down upon one side. Of course, his hands were at liberty, and with these he held a cross, which he displayed to the people as he rode along, and gave them his benediction.

After the patriarch, there followed, on these occasions, an immensely long train of priests, all clothed in costly and gorgeous sacerdotal robes, and bearing a great number and variety of religious emblems. Some carried very costly copies of the Gospels, bound in gold and adorned with precious stones; others crosses, and others pictures of the Virgin Mary. All these objects of veneration were enriched with jewels and gems of the most costly description.

So far, however, as these mere pageants and ceremonies were concerned, Peter would probably have been very easily satisfied, and would have made no objection to paying such a token of respect to the patriarch as walking before him through the street once a year, and holding the bridle of his horse, if this were all. But he saw very clearly that these things were by no means to be considered as mere outward show. The patriarch was at the head of a vast organization, which extended throughout the empire, all the members of which were closely banded together in a system the discipline of which made them dependent upon and entirely devoted to their spiritual head. These priests, moreover, exercised individually a vast influence over the people in the towns and villages where they severally lived and performed their functions. Thus the patriarch wielded a great and very extended power, almost wholly independent of any control on the part of the Czar—a power which had already been once turned against him, and which might at some future day become very dangerous. Peter determined at once that he would not allow such a state of things to continue.

He, however, resolved to proceed cautiously. So he waited quietly until the patriarch who was then in office died. Then, instead of allowing the bench of bishops, as usual, to elect another in his place, he committed the administration of the Church to an ecclesiastic whom he appointed for this purpose from among his own tried friends. He instructed this officer, who was a very learned and a very devout man, to go on as nearly as possible as his predecessors, the patriarchs, had done, in the ordinary routine of duty, so as not to disturb the Church by any apparent and outward change; but he directed him to consider himself, the Czar, as the real head of the Church, and to refer all important questions which might arise to him for decision. He thus, in fact, abrogated the office of patriarch, and made himself the supreme head of the Church.

The clergy throughout the empire, as soon as they understood this arrangement, were greatly disturbed, and expressed their discontent and dissatisfaction among themselves very freely. The Czar heard of this; and, selecting one of the bishops, who had spoken more openly and decidedly than the rest, he ordered him to be degraded from his office for his contumacy. But this the other bishops objected to very strongly. They did not see, in fact, they said, how it could be done. It was a thing wholly unknown that a person of the rank and dignity of a bishop in the Church should be degraded from his office; and that, besides, there was no authority that could degrade him, for they were all bishops of equal rank, and no one had any jurisdiction or power over the others. Still, notwithstanding this, they were willing, they said, to sacrifice their brother if by that means the Church could be saved from the great dangers which were now threatening her; and they said that they would depose the bishop who was accused on condition that Peter would restore the rights of the Church which he had suspended, by allowing them to proceed to the election of a new patriarch, to take the place of the one who had died.

Peter would not listen to this proposal; but he created a new bishop expressly to depose the one who had offended him. The latter was accordingly deposed, and the rest were compelled to submit. None of them dared any longer to speak openly against the course which the Czar was pursuing, but writings were mysteriously dropped about the streets which contained censures of his proceedings in respect to the Church, and urged the people to resist them. Peter caused large rewards to be immediately offered for the discovery of the persons by whom these writings were dropped, but it was of no avail, and at length the excitement gradually passed away, leaving the victory wholly in Peter's hands.

After this the Czar effected a great many important reforms in the administration of the affairs of the empire, especially in those relating to the government of the provinces, and to the collection of the revenues in them. This business had been hitherto left almost wholly in the hands of the governors, by whom it had been grossly mismanaged. The governors had been in the habit both of grievously oppressing the people in the collection of the taxes, and also of grossly defrauding the emperor in remitting the proceeds to the treasury.

Peter now made arrangements for changing the system entirely. He established a central office at the capital for the transaction of all business connected with the collecting of the revenues, and then appointed collectors for all the provinces of the empire, who were to receive their instructions from the minister who presided over this central office, and make their returns directly to him. Thus the whole system was remodeled, and made far more efficient than it ever had been before. Of course, the old governors, who, in consequence of this reform, lost the power of enriching themselves by their oppressions and frauds, complained bitterly of the change, and mourned, like good Conservatives, the ruin which this radicalism was bringing upon the country, but they were forced to submit.

Whenever there was any thing in the private manners and customs of the people which Peter thought was likely to impede in any way the effectual accomplishment of his plans, he did not hesitate at all to ordain a change; and some of the greatest difficulties which he had to encounter in his reforms arose from the opposition which the people made to the changes that he wished to introduce in the dress that they wore, and in several of the usages of common life. The people of the country had been accustomed to wear long gowns, similar to those worn to this day by many Oriental nations. This costume was very inconvenient, not only for soldiers, but also for workmen, and for all persons engaged in any of the common avocations of life. Peter required the people to change this dress; and he sent patterns of the coats worn in western Europe to all parts of the country, and had them put up in conspicuous places, where every body could see them, and required every body to imitate them. He, however, met with a great deal of difficulty in inducing them to do so. He found still greater difficulty in inducing the people to shave off their mustaches and their beards. Finding that they would not shave their faces under the influence of a simple regulation to that effect, he assessed a tax upon beards, requiring that every gentleman should pay a hundred rubles a year for the privilege of wearing one; and as for the peasants and common people, every one who wore a beard was stopped every time he entered a city or town, and required to pay a penny at the gate by way of tax or fine.

The nuisance of long clothes he attempted to abate in a similar way. The officers of the customs, who were stationed at the gates of the towns, were ordered to stop every man who wore a long dress, and compel him either to pay a fine of about fifty cents, or else kneel down and have all that part of their coat or gown which lay upon the ground, while they were in that posture, cut off with a pair of big shears.

Still, such was the attachment of the people to their old fashions, that great numbers of the people, rather than submit

Jacob Abbott

to this curtailing of their vestments, preferred to pay the fine.

On one occasion the Czar, laying aside for the moment the system of severity and terror which was his usual reliance for the accomplishment of his ends, concluded to try the effect of ridicule upon the attachment of the people to old and absurd fashions in dress. It happened that one of the fools or jesters of the court was about to be married. The young woman who was to be the jester's bride was very pretty, and she was otherwise a favorite with those who knew her, and the Czar determined to improve the occasion of the wedding for a grand frolic. He accordingly made arrangements for celebrating the nuptials at the palace, and he sent invitations to all the great nobles and officers of state, with their wives, and to all the other great ladies of the court, giving them all orders to appear dressed in the fashions which prevailed in the Russian court one or two hundred years before. With the exception of some modes of dress prevalent at the present day, there is nothing that can be conceived more awkward, inconvenient, and ridiculous than the fashions which were reproduced on this occasion. Among other things, the ladies wore a sort of dress of which the sleeves, so it is said, were ten or twelve yards long. These sleeves were made very full, and were drawn up upon the arm in a sort of a puff, it being the fashion to have as great a length to the sleeve as could possibly be crowded on between the shoulder and the wrist. It is said, too, that the customary salutation between ladies and gentlemen meeting in society, when this dress was in fashion, was performed through the intervention of these sleeves. On the approach of the gentleman, the lady, by a sudden and dexterous motion other arm, would throw off the end of her sleeve to him. The sleeve, being very long, could be thrown in this way half across the room. The gentleman would take the end of the sleeve, which represented, we are to suppose, the hand of the lady, and, after kissing and saluting it in a most respectful manner, he would resign it, and then the lady would draw it back again upon her arm. This would be too ridiculous to be believed if it were possible that any thing could be too ridiculous to be believed in respect to the absurdities of fashion.

A great many of the customs and usages of social life which prevailed in those days, as well as the fashions of dress, were inconvenient and absurd. These the Czar did not hesitate to alter and reform by proceedings of the most arbitrary and summary character. For instance, it was the custom of all the great nobles, or boyars, as they were called, to go in grand state whenever they moved about the city or in the environs of it, attended always by a long train of their servants and retainers. Now, as these followers were mostly on foot, the nobles in the carriages, or, in the winter, in their sledges or sleighs, were obliged to move very slowly in order to enable the train to keep up with them. Thus the streets were full of these tedious processions, moving slowly along, sometimes through snow and sometimes through rain, the men bareheaded, because they must not be covered in the presence of their master, and thus exposed to all the inclemency of an almost Arctic climate. And what made the matter worse was, that it was not the fashion for the nobleman to move on even as fast as his followers might easily have walked. They considered it more dignified and grand to go slowly. Thus, the more aristocratic a grandee was in spirit, and the greater his desire to make a display of his magnificence in the street, the more slowly he moved. If it had not been for the banners and emblems, and the gay and gaudy colors in which many of the attendants were dressed, these processions would have produced the effect of particularly solemn funerals.

The Czar determined to change all this. First he set an example himself of rapid motion through the streets. When he went out in his carriage or in his sleigh, he was attended only by a very few persons, and they were dressed in a neat uniform and mounted on good horses, and his coachman was ordered to drive on at a quick pace. The boyars were slow to follow this example, but the Czar assisted them considerably in their progress toward the desired reform by making rules limiting the number of idle attendants which they were allowed to have about them; and then, if they would not dismiss the supernumeraries, he himself caused them to be taken from them and sent into the army.

The motive of the Czar in making all these improvements and reforms was his desire to render his own power as the sovereign of the country more compact and efficient, and not any real and heartfelt interest in the welfare and happiness of the people. Still, in the end, very excellent results followed from the innovations which he thus introduced. They were the commencement of a series of changes which so developed the power and advanced the civilization of the country, as in the course of a few subsequent reigns had the effect of bringing Russia into the foremost rank among the nations of Europe. The progress which these changes introduced continues to go on to the present time, and will, perhaps, go on unimpeded for centuries to come.

[1] 1858.

CHAPTER X

THE BATTLE OF NARVA

1700-1701

Origin of the war with Sweden—Peace with the Turks—
Charles XII—Siege of Narva—The frontier—Plan of the
campaign—Indignation of the King of Sweden—
Remonstrances of Holland and England—The King of
Sweden at Riga—the Czar a subordinate—General Croy—
His plans—Operations of the king—Surprise and defeat of
the Russians—Terrible slaughter—Whimsical plan for
disposing of the prisoners—Effect upon the Czar—New
plans and arrangements

The reader will perhaps recollect how desirous Peter had
long been to extend his dominions toward the west, so as to
have a sea-port under his control on the Baltic Sea; for, at the
time when he succeeded to the throne, the eastern shores of
the Baltic belonged to Poland and to Sweden, so that the
Russians were confined, in a great measure, in their naval
operations to the waters of the Black and Caspian Seas, and
to the rivers flowing into them. You will also recollect that
when, at the commencement of his tour, he arrived at the
town of Riga, which stands at the head of the Gulf of Riga, a
sort of branch of the Baltic, he had been much offended at

the refusal of the governor of the place, acting under the orders of the King of Sweden, to allow him to view the fortifications there. He then resolved that Riga, and the whole province of which it was the capital, should one day be his. The year after he returned from his travels—that is, in 1699, the country being by that time restored to its ordinary state of repose after the suppression of the rebellion—he concluded that the time had arrived for carrying his resolution into effect.

So he set a train of negotiations on foot for making a long truce with the Turks, not wishing to have two wars on his hands at the same time. When he had accomplished this object, he formed a league with the kingdoms of Poland and Denmark to make war upon Sweden. So exactly were all his plans laid, that the war with Sweden was declared on the very next day after the truce of the Turks was concluded.

The King of Sweden at this time was Charles XII. He was a mere boy, being only at that time eighteen years of age, and he had just succeeded to the throne. He was, however, a prince of remarkable talents and energy, and in his subsequent campaigns against Peter and his allies he distinguished himself so much that he acquired great renown, and finally took his place among the most illustrious military heroes in history.

The first operation of the war was the siege of the city of Narva. Narva was a port on the Baltic; the situation of it, as well as that of the other places mentioned in this chapter, is seen by the adjoining map, which shows the general features of the Russian and Swedish frontier as it existed at that time.

Narva, as appears by the map, is situated on the sea-coast, near the frontier—much nearer than Riga. Peter expected that by the conquest of this city he should gain access to the sea, and so be able to build ships which would aid him in his ulterior operations. He also calculated that when Narva was in his hands the way would be open for him to advance on Riga. Indeed, at the same time while he was commencing the siege of Narva, his ally, the King of Poland, advanced from his own dominions to Riga, and was now prepared to attack that city at the same time that the Czar was besieging Narva.

In the mean while the news of these movements was sent by couriers to the King of Sweden, and the conduct of Peter in thus suddenly making war upon him, and invading his dominions, made him exceedingly indignant. The only cause of quarrel which Peter pretended to have against the king was the uncivil treatment which he had received at the hands of the Governor of Riga in refusing to allow him to see the fortifications when he passed through that city on his tour. Peter had, it is true, complained of this insult, as he called it, and had sent commissioners to Sweden to demand satisfaction; and certain explanations had been made, though Peter professed not to be satisfied with them. Still, the negotiations had not been closed, and the government of Sweden had no idea that the misunderstanding would lead to war. Indeed, the commissioners were still at the Swedish court, continuing the negotiations, when the news arrived that Peter had at once brought the question to an issue by declaring war and invading the Swedish territory. The king immediately collected a large army, and provided a fleet of two hundred transports to convey them to the scene of action. The preparations were made with great dispatch, and the fleet sailed for Riga.

The news, too, of this war occasioned great dissatisfaction among the governments of western Europe. The government of Holland was particularly displeased, on account of the interference and interruption which the war would occasion to all their commerce in the Baltic. They immediately determined to remonstrate with the Czar against the course which he was pursuing, and they induced King William, of England, to join them in the remonstrance. They also, at the same time, sent a messenger to the King of Poland, urging him by all means to suspend his threatened attack on Riga until some measures could be taken for accommodating the quarrel. Riga was a very important commercial port, and there were a great many wealthy Dutch merchants there, whose interests the Dutch government were very anxious to protect.

The King of Sweden arrived at Riga with his fleet at just about the same time that the remonstrance of the Dutch government reached the King of Poland, who was advancing to attack it. Augustus, for that was the name of the King of Poland, finding that now, since so great a force had arrived to succor and strengthen the place, there was no hope for success in any of his operations against it, concluded to make a virtue of necessity, and so he drew off his army, and sent word to the Dutch government that he did so in compliance with their wishes.

The King of Sweden had, of course, nothing now to do but to advance from Riga to Narva and attack the army of the Czar.

This army was not, however, commanded by the Czar in person. In accordance with what seems to have been his favorite plan in all his great undertakings, he did not act directly himself as the head of the expedition, but, putting forward another man, an experienced and skillful general, as responsible commander, he himself took a subordinate position as lieutenant. Indeed, he took a pride in entering the army at one of the very lowest grades, and so advancing, by a regular series of promotions, through all the ranks of the service. The person whom the Czar had made commander-in-chief at the siege of Narva was a German officer. His name was General Croy.

General Croy had been many weeks before Narva at the time when the King of Sweden arrived at Riga, but he had made little progress in taking the town. The place was strongly fortified, and the garrison, though comparatively weak, defended it with great bravery. The Russian army was encamped in a very strong position just outside the town. As soon as news of the coming of the King of Sweden arrived, the Czar went off into the interior of the country to hasten a large re-enforcement which had been ordered, and, at the same time, General Croy sent forward large bodies of men to lay in ambuscade along the roads and defiles through which the King of Sweden would have to pass on his way from Riga.

But all these excellent arrangements were entirely defeated by the impetuous energy, and the extraordinary tact and skill of the King of Sweden. Although his army was very much smaller than that of the Russians, he immediately set out on his march to Narva; but, instead of moving along the regular roads, and so falling into the ambuscade which the Russians had laid for him, he turned off into back and circuitous by-ways, so as to avoid the snare altogether. It was in the dead of winter, and the roads which he followed, besides being rough and intricate, were obstructed with snow, and the Russians had thought little of them, so that at last, when the Swedish army arrived at their advanced posts, they were taken entirely by surprise. The advanced posts were driven in, and the Swedes pressed on, the Russians flying before them, and carrying confusion to the posts in the rear. The surprise of the Russians, and the confusion consequent upon it, were greatly increased by the state of the weather; for there was a violent snow-storm at the time, and the snow, blowing into the Russians' faces, prevented their seeing what the numbers were of the enemy so suddenly assaulting them,

Jacob Abbott

or taking any effectual measures to restore their own ranks to order when once deranged.

When at length the Swedes, having thus driven in the advanced posts, reached the Russian camp itself, they immediately made an assault upon it. The camp was defended by a rampart and by a double ditch, but on went the assaulting soldiers over all the obstacles, pushing their way with their bayonets, and carrying all before them. The Russians were entirely defeated and put to flight.

In a rout like this, the conquering army, maddened by rage and by all the other dreadful excitements of the contest, press on furiously upon their flying and falling foes, and destroy them with their bayonets in immense numbers before the officers can arrest them. Indeed, the officers do not wish to arrest them until it is sure that the enemy is so completely overwhelmed that their rallying again is utterly impossible. In this case twenty thousand of the Russian soldiers were left dead upon the field. The Swedes, on the other hand, lost only two or three thousand.

Besides those who were killed, immense numbers were taken prisoners. General Croy, and all the other principal generals in command, were among the prisoners. It is very probable that, if Peter had not been absent at the time, he would himself have been taken too.

The number of prisoners was so very great that it was not possible for the Swedes to retain them, on account of the expense and trouble of feeding them, and keeping them warm at that season of the year; so they determined to detain the officers only, and to send the men away. In doing this, besides disarming the men, they adopted a very whimsical expedient for making them helpless and incapable of doing mischief on their march. They cut their clothes in such a manner that they could only be prevented from falling off by being held together by both hands; and the weather was so cold—the ground, moreover, being covered with snow—that the men could only save themselves from perishing by keeping their clothes around them.

In this pitiful plight the whole body of prisoners were driven off, like a flock of sheep, by a small body of Swedish soldiery, for a distance of about a league on the road toward Russia, and then left to find the rest of the way themselves.

The Czar, when he heard the news of this terrible disaster, did not seem much disconcerted by it. He said that he expected to be beaten at first by the Swedes. "They have beaten us once," said he, "and they may beat us again; but they will teach us in time to beat them."

He immediately began to adopt the most efficient and energetic measures for organizing a new army. He set about raising recruits in all parts of the empire. He introduced many new foreign officers into his service; and to provide artillery, after exhausting all the other resources at his command, he ordered the great bells of many churches and monasteries to be taken down and cast into cannon.

CHAPTER XI

THE BUILDING OF ST. PETERSBURG

1700-1704

Continuation of the war—Stratagems of the Swedes—Peculiar kind of boat—Making a smoke—Peter determines to build a city—The site—Peter's first visit to the Neva—Cronstadt—A stratagem—Contest on the island—Peter examines the locality—He matures his plans—Mechanics and artisans—Ships and merchandise—Laborers—The boyars—The building commenced—Wharves and piers—Palace—Confusion—Variety of labors—Want of tools and implements—Danger from the enemy—Supplies of provisions—The supplies often fall short—Consequent sickness—Great mortality—Peter's impetuosity of spirit—Streets and buildings—Private dwellings—What the King of Sweden said—Map—Situation of Cronstadt—Peter plans a fortress—Mode of laying the foundations—Danger from the Swedes—Plan of their attack—The Swedes beaten off—The attempt entirely fails—Mechanics and artisans—Various improvements—Scientific institutions

The struggle thus commenced between the Czar Peter and Charles XII. of Sweden, for the possession of the eastern shores of the Baltic Sea, continued for many years. At first the Russians were every where beaten by the Swedes; but at last, as Peter had predicted, the King of Sweden taught them to beat him.

The commanders of the Swedish army were very ingenious in expedients, as well as bold and energetic in action, and they often gained an advantage over their enemy by their wit as well as by their bravery. One instance of this was their contrivance for rendering their prisoners helpless on their march homeward after the battle of Narva, by cutting their clothes in such a manner as to compel the men to keep both hands employed, as they walked along the roads, in holding them together. On another occasion, when they had to cross a river in the face of the Russian troops posted on the other side, they invented a peculiar kind of boat, which was of great service in enabling them to accomplish the transit in safety. These boats were flat-bottomed and square; the foremost end of each of them was guarded by a sort of bulwark, formed of plank, and made very high. This bulwark was fixed on hinges at the lower end, so that it could be raised up and down. It was, of course, kept up during the passage across the river, and so served to defend the men in the boat from the shots of the enemy. But when the boat reached the shore it was let down, and then it formed a platform or bridge by which the men could all rush out together to the shore.

At the same time, while they were getting these boats ready, and placing the men in them, the Swedes, having observed that the wind blew across from their side of the river to the other, made great fires on the bank, and covered them with wet straw, so as to cause them to throw out a prodigious quantity of smoke. The smoke was blown over to the other side of the river, where it so filled the air as to prevent the Russians from seeing what was going on.

Jacob Abbott

It was about a year after the first breaking out of the war that the tide of fortune began to turn, in some measure, in favor of the Russians. About that time the Czar gained possession of a considerable portion of the Baltic shore; and as soon as he had done so, he conceived the design of laying the foundation of a new city there, with the view of making it the naval and commercial capital of his kingdom. This plan was carried most successfully into effect in the building of the great city of St. Petersburg. The founding of this city was one of the most important transactions in Peter's reign. Indeed, it was probably by far the most important, and Peter owes, perhaps, more of his great fame to this memorable enterprise than to any thing else that he did.

The situation of St. Petersburg will be seen by the map in the preceding chapter. At a little distance from the shore is a large lake, called the Lake of Ladoga. The outlet of the Lake of Ladoga is a small river called the Neva. The Lake of Ladoga is supplied with water by many rivers, which flow into it from the higher lands lying to the northward and eastward of it; and it is by the Neva that the surplus of these waters is carried off to the sea.

The circumstances under which the attention of the Czar was called to the advantages of this locality were these. He arrived on the banks of the Neva, at some distance above the mouth of the river, in the course of his campaign against the Swedes in the year 1702. He followed the river down, and observed that it was pretty wide, and that the water was sufficiently deep for the purpose of navigation. When he reached the mouth of the river, he saw that, there was an island,[1] at some distance from the shore, which might easily be fortified, and that, when fortified, it would completely defend the entrance to the stream. He took with him a body of armed men, and went off to the island in boats, in order to examine it more closely. The name of this island was then almost unknown, but it is now celebrated throughout the world as the seat of the renowned and impregnable fortress of Cronstadt.

There was a Swedish ship in the offing at the time when Peter visited the island, and this ship drew near to the island and began to fire upon it as soon as those on board saw that the Russian soldiers had landed there. This cannonading drove the Russians back from the shores, but instead of retiring from the island they went and concealed themselves behind some rocks. The Swedes supposed that the Russians had gone around to the other side of the island, and that they had there taken to their boats again and returned to the main land; so they determined to go to the island themselves, and examine it, in order to find out what the Russians had been doing there.

They accordingly let down their boats, and a large party of Swedes embarking in them rowed to the island. Soon after they had landed the Russians rushed out upon them from their ambuscade, and, after a sharp contest, drove them back to their boats. Several of the men were killed, but the rest succeeded in making their way to the ship, and the ship soon afterward weighed anchor and put to sea.

Peter was now at liberty to examine the island, the mouth of the river, and all the adjacent shores, as much as he pleased. He found that the situation of the place was well adapted to the purposes of a sea-port. The island would serve to defend the mouth of the river, and yet there was deep water along the side of it to afford an entrance for ships. The water, too, was deep in the river, and the flow of the current smooth. It is true that in many places the land along the banks of the river was low and marshy, but this difficulty could be remedied by the driving of piles for the foundation of the buildings, which had been done so extensively in Holland.

Jacob Abbott

There was no town on the spot at the time of Peter's visit to it, but only a few fishermen's huts near the outlet of the river, and the ruins of an old fort a few miles above. Peter examined the whole region with great care, and came decidedly to the conclusion that he would make the spot the site of a great city.

He matured his plans during the winter, and in the following spring he commenced the execution of them. The first building that was erected was a low one-story structure, made of wood, to be used as a sort of office and place of shelter for himself while superintending the commencement of the works that he had projected. This building was afterward preserved a long time with great care, as a precious relic and souvenir of the foundation of the city.

The Czar had sent out orders to the governments of the different provinces of the empire requiring each of them to send his quota of artificers and laborers to assist in building the city. This they could easily do, for in those days all the laboring classes of the people were little better than slaves, and were almost entirely at the disposal of the nobles, their masters. In the same manner he sent out agents to all the chief cities in western Europe, with orders to advertise there for carpenters, masons, engineers, ship-builders, and persons of all the other trades likely to be useful in the work of building the city. These men were to be promised good wages and kind treatment, and were to be at liberty at any time to return to their respective homes.

The agents also, at the same time, invited the merchants of the countries that they visited to send vessels to the new port, laden with food for the people that were to be assembled there, and implements for work, and other merchandise suitable for the wants of such a community. The merchants were promised good prices for their goods, and full liberty to come and go at their pleasure.

The Czar also sent orders to a great many leading boyars or nobles, requiring them to come and build houses for themselves in the new town. They were to bring with them a sufficient number of their serfs and retainers to do all the rough work which would be required, and money to pay the foreign mechanics for the skilled labor. The boyars were not at all pleased with this summons. They already possessed their town houses in Moscow, with gardens and pleasure-grounds in the environs. The site for the new city was very far to the northward, in a comparatively cold and inhospitable climate; and they knew very well that, even if Peter should succeed, in the end, in establishing his new city, several years must elapse before they could live there in comfort. Still, they did not dare to do otherwise than to obey the emperor's summons.

In consequence of all these arrangements and preparations, immense numbers of people came in to the site of the new city in the course of the following spring and summer. The numbers were swelled by the addition of the populations of many towns and villages along the coast that had been ravaged or destroyed by the Swedes in the course of the war. The works were immediately commenced on a vast scale, and they were carried on during the summer with great energy. The first thing to be secured was, of course, the construction of the fortress which was to defend the town. There were wharves and piers to be built too, in order that the vessels bringing stores and provisions might land their goods. The land was surveyed, streets laid out, building lots assigned to merchants for warehouses and shops, and to the boyars for palaces and gardens. The boyars commenced the building of their houses, and the Czar himself laid the foundation of an imperial palace.

But, notwithstanding all the precautions which Peter had taken to secure supplies of every thing required for such an undertaking, and to regulate the work by systematic plans and arrangements, the operations were for a time attended with a great deal of disorder and confusion, and a vast amount of personal suffering. For a long time there was no proper shelter for the laborers. Men came to the ground much faster than huts could be built to cover them, and they were obliged to lie on the marshy ground without any protection from the weather. There was also a great scarcity of tools and implements suitable for the work that was required, in felling and transporting trees, and in excavating and filling up, where changes in the surface were required. In constructing the fortifications, for example, which, in the first instance, were made of earth, it was necessary to dig deep ditches and to raise great embankments. There was a great deal of the same kind of work necessary on the ground where the city was to stand before the work of erecting buildings could be commenced. There were dikes and levees to be made along the margin of the stream to protect the land from the inundations to which it was subject when the river was swollen with rains. There were roads to be made, and forests to be cleared away, and many other such labors to be performed. Now, in order to employ at once the vast concourse of laborers that were assembled on the ground in such works as these, an immense number of implements were required, such as pickaxes, spades, shovels, and wheelbarrows; but so limited was the supply of these conveniences, that a great portion of the earth which was required for the dikes and embankments was brought by the men in their aprons, or in the skirts of their clothes, or in bags made for the purpose out of old mats, or any other material that came to hand. It was necessary to push forward the work promptly and without any delay, notwithstanding all these disadvantages, for the Swedes were still off the coast with their ships, and no one knew how soon they might draw near and open a cannonade upon the place, or even land and attack the workmen in the midst of their labors.

What greatly increased the difficulties of the case was the frequent falling short of the supply of provisions. The number of men to be fed was immensely large; for, in consequence of the very efficient measures which the Czar had taken for gathering men from all parts of his dominions, it is said that there were not less than three hundred thousand collected on the spot in the course of the summer. And as there were at that time no roads leading to the place, all the supplies were necessarily to be brought by water. But the approach from the Baltic side was well-nigh cut off by the Swedes, who had at that time full possession of the sea. Vessels could, however, come from the interior by way of Lake Ladoga; but when for several days or more the wind was from the west, these vessels were all kept back, and then sometimes the provisions fell short, and the men were reduced to great distress. To guard as much as possible against the danger of coming to absolute want at the times when the supplies were thus entirely cut off, the men were often put on short allowance beforehand. The emperor, it is true, was continually sending out requisitions for more food; but the men increased in number faster, after all, than the means for feeding them. The consequence was, that immense multitudes of them sickened and died. The scarcity of food, combined with the influence of fatigue and exposure—men half fed, working all day in the mud and rain, and at night sleeping without any shelter—brought on fevers and dysenteries, and other similar diseases, which always prevail in camps, and among large bodies of men exposed to such influences as these. It is said that not less than a hundred thousand men perished from these causes at St. Petersburg in the course of the year.

Peter doubtless regretted this loss of life, as it tended to

Jacob Abbott

impede the progress of the work; but, after all, it was a loss which he could easily repair by sending out continually to the provinces for fresh supplies of men. Those whom the nobles and governors selected from among the serfs and ordered to go had no option; they were obliged to submit. And thus the supply of laborers was kept full, notwithstanding the dreadful mortality which was continually tending to diminish it.

If Peter had been willing to exercise a little patience and moderation in carrying out his plans, it is very probable that most of this suffering might have been saved. If he had sent a small number of men to the ground the first year, and had employed them in opening roads, establishing granaries, and making other preliminary arrangements, and, in the mean time, had caused stores of food to be purchased and laid up, and ample supplies of proper tools and implements to be procured and conveyed to the ground, so as to have had every thing ready for the advantageous employment of a large number of men in the following year, every thing would, perhaps, have gone well. But the qualities of patience and moderation formed no part of Peter's character. What he conceived of and determined to do must be done at once, at whatever cost; and a cost of human life seems to have been the one that he thought less of than any other. He rushed headlong on, notwithstanding the suffering which his impetuosity occasioned, and thus the hymn which solemnized the entrance into being of the new-born city was composed of the groans of a hundred thousand men, dying in agony, of want, misery, and despair.

Peter was a personal witness of this suffering, for he remained, during a great part of the time, on the ground, occupying himself constantly in superintending and urging on the operations. Indeed, it is said that he acted himself as chief engineer in planning the fortifications, and in laying out the streets of the city. He drew many of the plans with his own hands; for, among the other accomplishments which he had acquired in the early part of his life, he had made himself quite a good practical draughtsman.

When the general plan of the city had been determined upon, and proper places had been set apart for royal palaces and pleasure-grounds, and public edifices of all sorts that might be required, and also for open squares, docks, markets, and the like, a great many streets were thrown open for the use of any persons who might choose to build houses in them. A vast number of the mechanics and artisans who had been attracted to the place by the offers of the Czar availed themselves of this opportunity to provide themselves with homes, and they proceeded at once to erect houses. A great many of the structures thus built were mere huts or shanties, made of any rude materials that came most readily to hand, and put up in a very hasty manner. It was sufficient that the tenement afforded a shelter from the rain, and that it was enough of a building to fulfill the condition on which the land was granted to the owner of it. The number of these structures was, however, enormous. It was said that in one year there were erected thirty thousand of them. There is no instance in the history of the world of so great a city springing into existence with such marvelous rapidity as this.

During the time while Peter was thus employed in laying the foundations of his new city, the King of Sweden was carrying on the war in Poland against the conjoined forces of Russia and Poland, which were acting together there as allies. When intelligence was brought to him of the operations in which Peter was engaged on the banks of the Neva, he said, "It is all very well. He may amuse himself as much as he likes in building his city there; but by-and-by, when I am a little at leisure, I will go and take it away from him. Then, if I like the town, I will keep it; and if not, I will burn it down."

Peter, however, determined that it should not be left within the power of the King of Sweden to take his town, or even to molest his operations in the building of it, if any precautions on his part could prevent it. He had caused a number of redoubts and batteries to be thrown up during the summer. These works were situated at different points near the outlet of the river, and on the adjacent shores.

There was an island off the mouth of the river which stood in a suitable position to guard the entrance. This island was several miles distant from the place where the city was to stand, and it occupied the middle of the bay leading toward it. Thus there was water on both sides of it, but the water was deep enough only on one side to allow of the passage of ships of war. Peter now determined to construct a large and strong fortress on the shores of this island, placing it in such a position that the guns could command the channel leading up the bay. It was late in the fall when he planned this work, and the winter came on before he was ready to commence operations. This time for commencing was, however, a matter of design on his part, as the ice during the winter would assist very much, he thought, in the work of laying the necessary foundations; for the fortress was not to stand on the solid land, but on a sandbank which projected from the land on the side toward the navigable channel. The site of the fortress was to be about a cannon-shot from the and, where, being surrounded by shallow water on every side, it could not be approached either by land or sea.

Peter laid the foundations of this fortress on the ice by building immense boxes of timber and plank, and loading them with stones. When the ice melted in the spring these structures sank into the sand, and formed a stable and solid foundation on which he could afterward build at pleasure.

This was the origin of the famous Castle of Cronstadt, which has since so well fulfilled its purpose that it has kept the powerful navies of Europe at bay in time of war, and prevented their reaching the city.

Besides this great fortress, Peter erected several detached batteries at different parts of the island, so as to prevent the land from being approached at all by the boats of the enemy.

At length the King of Sweden began to be somewhat alarmed at the accounts which he received of what Peter was doing, and he determined to attack him on the ground, and destroy his works before he proceeded any farther with them. He accordingly ordered the admiral of the fleet to assemble his ships, to sail up the Gulf of Finland, and there attack and destroy the settlement which Peter was making.

The admiral made the attempt, but he found that he was too late. The works were advanced too far, and had become too strong for him. It was on the 4th of July, 1704, that the Russian scouts, who were watching on the shores of the bay, saw the Swedish ships coming up. The fleet consisted of twenty-two men-of-war, and many other vessels. Besides the forts and batteries, the Russians had a number of ships of their own at anchor in the waters, and as the fleet advanced a tremendous cannonade was opened on both sides, the ships of the Swedes against the ships and batteries of the Russians. When the Swedish fleet had advanced as far toward the island as the depth of the water would allow, they let down from the decks of their vessels a great number of flat-bottomed boats, which they had brought for the purpose, and filled them with armed men. Their plan was to land these men on the island, and carry the Russian batteries there at the point of the bayonet.

Jacob Abbott

But they did not succeed. They were received so hotly by the Russians that, after an obstinate contest, they were forced to retreat. They endeavored to get back to their boats, but were pursued by the Russians; and now, as their backs were turned, they could no longer defend themselves, and a great many were killed. Even those that were not killed did not all succeed in making their escape. A considerable number, finding that they should not be able to get to the boats, threw down their arms, and surrendered themselves prisoners; and then, of course, the boats which they belonged to were taken. Five of the boats thus fell into the hands of the Russians. The others were rowed back with all speed to the ships, and then the ships withdrew. Thus the attempt failed entirely. The admiral reported the ill success of his expedition to the king, and not long afterward another similar attempt was made, but with no better success than before.

The new city was now considered as firmly established, and from this time it advanced very rapidly in wealth and population. Peter gave great encouragement to foreign mechanics and artisans to come and settle in the town, offering to some lands, to others houses, and to others high wages for their work. The nobles built elegant mansions there in the streets set apart for them, and many public buildings of great splendor were planned and commenced. The business of building ships, too, was introduced on an extended scale. The situation was very favorable for this purpose, as the shores of the river afforded excellent sites for dock-yards, and the timber required could be supplied in great quantities from the shores of Lake Ladoga.

In a very few years after the first foundation of the city, Peter began to establish literary and scientific institutions there. Many of these institutions have since become greatly renowned, and they contribute a large share, at the present day, to the *eclat* which surrounds this celebrated city, and which makes it one of the most splendid and renowned of the European capitals.

[1] See map on page 221.

Jacob Abbott

CHAPTER XII

THE REVOLT OF MAZEPPA

1708

Progress of the war—Peter's fleet—The King of Sweden's successes—Peter wishes to make peace—The reply—Plan changed—Mazeppa and the Cossacks—Plans for reforming the Cossacks—Mazeppa opposes them—The quarrel—Mazeppa's treasonable designs—The plot defeated—Precautions of the Czar—Mazeppa's plans—He goes on step by step—He sends his nephew to the Czar—The envoy is arrested—Commotion among the Cossacks—Failure of the plot—Mazeppa's trial and condemnation—The effigy—Execution of the sentence upon the effigy—New chieftain chosen

In the mean time the war with Sweden went on. Many campaigns were fought, for the contest was continued through several successive years. The King of Sweden made repeated attempts to destroy the new city of St. Petersburg, but without success. On the contrary, the town grew and prospered more and more; and the shelter and protection which the fortifications around it afforded to the mouth of the river and to the adjacent roadsteads enabled the Czar to go on so rapidly in building new ships, and in thus increasing and strengthening his fleet, that very soon he was much stronger than the King of Sweden in all the neighboring waters, so that he not only was able to keep the enemy very effectually at bay, but he even made several successful descents upon the Swedish territory along the adjoining coasts.

But, while the Czar was thus rapidly increasing his power at sea, the King of Sweden proved himself the strongest on land. He extended his conquests very rapidly in Poland and in the adjoining provinces, and at last, in the summer of 1708, he conceived the design of crossing the Dnieper and threatening Moscow, which was still Peter's capital. He accordingly pushed his forces forward until he approached the bank of the river. He came up to it at a certain point, as if he was intending to cross there. Peter assembled all his troops on the opposite side of the river at that point in order to oppose him. But the demonstration which the king made of an intention to cross at that point was only a pretense. He left a sufficient number of men there to make a show, and secretly marched away the great body of his troops in the night to a point about three miles farther up the river, where he succeeded in crossing with them before the emperor's forces had any suspicion of his real design. The Russians, who were not strong enough to oppose him in the open field, were obliged immediately to retreat, and leave him in full possession of the ground.

Peter was now much alarmed. He sent an officer to the camp of the King of Sweden with a flag of truce, to ask on what terms the king would make peace with him. But Charles was too much elated with his success in crossing the river, and placing himself in a position from which he could advance, without encountering any farther obstruction, to the very gates of the capital, to be willing then to propose any terms. So he declined entering into any negotiation, saying only in a haughty tone "that he would treat with his brother Peter at Moscow."

On mature reflection, however, he seems to have concluded that it would be more prudent for him not to march at once to Moscow, and so he turned his course for a time toward the southward, in the direction of the Crimea and the Black Sea.

There was one secret reason which induced the King of Sweden to move thus to the southward which Peter did not for a time understand. The country of the Cossacks lay in that direction, and the famous Mazeppa, of whom some account has already been given in this volume, was the chieftain of the Cossacks, and he, as it happened, had had a quarrel with the Czar, and in consequence of it had opened a secret negotiation with the King of Sweden, and had agreed that if the king would come into his part of the country he would desert the cause of the Czar, and would come over to his side, with all the Cossacks under his command.

The cause of Mazeppa's quarrel with the Czar was this: He was one day paying a visit to his majesty, and, while seated at table, Peter began to complain of the lawless and ungovernable character of the Cossacks, and to propose that Mazeppa should introduce certain reforms in the organization and discipline of the tribe, with a view of bringing them under more effectual control. It is probable that the reforms which he proposed were somewhat analogous to those which he had introduced so successfully into the armies under his own more immediate command.

Mazeppa opposed this suggestion. He said that the attempt to adopt such measures with the Cossacks would never succeed; that the men were so wild and savage by nature, and so fixed in the rude and irregular habits of warfare to which they and their fathers had been so long accustomed, that they could never be made to submit to such restrictions as a regular military discipline would impose.

Peter, who never could endure the least opposition or contradiction to any of his ideas or plans, became quite angry with Mazeppa on account of the objections which he made to his proposals, and, as was usual with him in such cases, he broke out in the most rude and violent language imaginable. He called Mazeppa an enemy and a traitor, and threatened to have him impaled alive. It is true he did not really mean what he said, his words being only empty threats dictated by the brutal violence of his anger. Still, Mazeppa was very much offended. He went away from the Czar's tent muttering his displeasure, and resolving secretly on revenge.

Soon after this Mazeppa opened the communication above referred to with the King of Sweden, and at last an agreement was made between them by which it was stipulated that the king was to advance into the southern part of the country, where, of course, the Cossacks would be sent out to meet him, and then Mazeppa was to revolt from the Czar, and go over with all his forces to the King of Sweden's side. By this means the Czar's army was sure, they thought, to be defeated; and in this case the King of Sweden was to remain in possession of the Russian territory, while the Cossacks were to retire to their own fortresses, and live thenceforth as an independent tribe.

The plot seemed to be very well laid; but, unfortunately for the contrivers of it, it was not destined to succeed. In the first place, Mazeppa's scheme of revolting with the Cossacks to the enemy was discovered by the Czar, and almost entirely defeated, before the time arrived for putting it into execution. Peter had his secret agents every where, and through them he received such information in respect to Mazeppa's movements as led him to suspect his designs. He said nothing, however, but manoeuvred his forces so as to have a large body of troops that he could rely upon always near Mazeppa and the Cossacks, and between them and the army of the Swedes. He ordered the officers of these troops to watch Mazeppa's movements closely, and to be ready to act against him at a moment's notice, should occasion require. Mazeppa was somewhat disconcerted in his plans by this state of things; but he could not make any objection, for the troops thus stationed near him seemed to be placed there for the purpose of co-operating with him against the enemy.

In the mean time, Mazeppa cautiously made known his plans to the leading men among the Cossacks as fast as he thought it prudent to do so. He represented to them how much better it would be for them to be restored to their former liberty as an independent tribe, instead of being in subjugation to such a despot as the Czar. He also enumerated the various grievances which they suffered under Russian rule, and endeavored to excite the animosity of his hearers as much as possible against Peter's government.

He found that the chief officers of the Cossacks seemed quite disposed to listen to what he said, and to adopt his views. Some of them were really so, and others pretended to be so for fear of displeasing him. At length he thought it time to take some measures for preparing the minds of the men generally for what was to come, and in order to do this he determined on publicly sending a messenger to the Czar with the complaints which he had to make in behalf of his men. The men, knowing of this embassy, and understanding the grounds of the complaint which Mazeppa was to make by means of it, would be placed, he thought, in such a position that, in the event of an unfavorable answer being returned, as he had no doubt would be the case, they could be the more easily led into the revolt which he proposed.

Mazeppa accordingly made out a statement of his complaints, and appointed his nephew a commissioner to proceed to head-quarters and lay them before the Czar. The name of the nephew was Warnarowski. As soon as Warnarowski arrived at the camp, Peter, instead of granting him an audience, and listening to the statement which he had to make, ordered him to be seized and sent to prison, as if he were guilty of a species of treason in coming to trouble his sovereign with complaints and difficulties at such a time, when the country was suffering under an actual invasion from a foreign enemy.

As soon as Mazeppa heard that his nephew was arrested, he was convinced that his plots had been discovered, and that he must not lose a moment in carrying them into execution, or all would be lost. He accordingly immediately put his whole force in motion to march toward the place where the Swedish army was then posted, ostensibly for the purpose of attacking them. He crossed a certain river which lay between him and the Swedes, and then, when safely over, he stated to his men what he intended to do.

The men were filled with indignation at this proposal, which, being wholly unexpected, came upon them by surprise. They refused to join in the revolt. A scene of great excitement and confusion followed. A portion of the Cossacks, those with whom Mazeppa had come to an understanding beforehand, were disposed to go with him, but the rest were filled with vexation and rage. They declared that they would seize their chieftain, bind him hand and foot, and send him to the Czar. Indeed, it is highly probable that the two factions would have come soon to a bloody fight for the possession of the person of their chieftain, in which case he would very likely have been torn to pieces in the struggle, if those who were disposed to revolt had not fled before the opposition to their movement had time to become organized. Mazeppa and those who adhered to him—about two thousand men in all—went over in a body to the camp of the Swedes. The rest, led by the officers that still remained faithful, marched at once to the nearest body of Russian forces, and put themselves under the command of the Russian general there.

A council of war was soon after called in the Russian camp for the purpose of bringing Mazeppa to trial. He was, of course, found guilty, and sentence of death—with a great many indignities to accompany the execution—was passed upon him. The sentence, however, could not be executed upon Mazeppa himself, for he was out of the reach of his accusers, being safe in the Swedish camp. So they made a wooden image or effigy to represent him, and inflicted the penalties upon the substitute instead.

In the first place, they dressed the effigy to imitate the appearance of Mazeppa, and put upon it representations of the medals, ribbons, and other decorations which he was accustomed to wear. They brought this figure out before the camp, in presence of the general and of all the leading officers, the soldiers being also drawn up around the spot. A herald appeared and read the sentence of condemnation, and then proceeded to carry it into execution, as follows. First, he tore Mazeppa's patent of knighthood in pieces, and threw the fragments into the air. Then he tore off the medals and decorations from the image, and, throwing them upon the ground, he trampled them under his feet. Then he struck the effigy itself a blow by which it was overturned and left prostrate in the dust.

The hangman then came up, and, tying a halter round the neck of the effigy, dragged it off to a place where a gibbet had been erected, and hanged it there.

Immediately after this ceremony, the Cossacks, according to

their custom, proceeded to elect a new chieftain in the place of Mazeppa. The chieftain thus chosen came forward before the Czar to take the oath of allegiance to him, and to offer him his homage.

Jacob Abbott

CHAPTER XIII

THE BATTLE OF PULTOWA

1709

Invasion of the Swedes—Their progress through the country—Artificial roads—Pultowa—Fame of the battle—Situation of Pultowa—It is besieged—Menzikoff—Manoeuvres—Menzikoff most successful—King Charles wounded—The Czar advances to Pultowa—The king resolves to attack the camp—A battle determined upon—Military rank of the Czar—His address to the army—The litter—The battle—Courage and fortitude of the king—The Swedes defeated—Narrow escape of the Czar—He discovers the broken litter—Escape of King Charles—Dreadful defeat—Flight and adventures of the king—He offers now to make peace—The king's followers—Peter's reply—Carriage for the king—Flight to the Turkish frontier—Sufferings of the retreating army—Deputation sent to the Turkish frontier—Reception of the messenger—Boats collected—Crossing the river—Bender—Fate of the Swedish army—The prisoners—Anecdote of the Czar—The Czar's habits—Disposition of the prisoners—Adventures of the King of Sweden—Military promotion of the Czar

In the mean time, while these transactions had been taking

place among the Russians, the King of Sweden had been gradually making his way toward the westward and southward, into the very heart of the Russian dominions. The forces of the emperor, which were not strong enough to offer him battle, had been gradually retiring before him; but they had devastated and destroyed every thing on their way, in their retreat, so as to leave nothing for the support of the Swedish army. They broke up all the bridges too, and obstructed the roads by every means in their power, so as to impede the progress of the Swedes as much as possible, since they could not wholly arrest it.

The Swedes, however, pressed slowly onward. They sent off to great distances to procure forage for the horses and food for the men. When they found the bridges down, they made detours and crossed the rivers at fording-places. When the roads were obstructed, they removed the impediments if they could, and if not, they opened new roads. Sometimes, in these cases, their way led them across swampy places where no solid footing could be found, and then the men would cut down an immense quantity of bushes and trees growing in the neighborhood, and make up the branches into bundles called *fascines*. They would lay these bundles close together on the surface of the swamp, and then level them off on the top by loose branches, and so make a road firm enough for the army to march over.

Things went on in this way until, at last, the farther progress of King Charles was arrested, and the tide of fortune was turned wholly against him by a great battle which was fought at a place called Pultowa. This battle, which, after so protracted a struggle, at length suddenly terminated the contest between the king and the Czar, of course attracted universal attention at the time, for Charles and Peter were the greatest potentates and warriors of their age, and the struggle for power which had so long been waged between them had been watched with great interest, through all the stages of it, by the whole civilized world. The battle of Pultowa was, in a word, one of those great final conflicts by which, after a long struggle, the fate of an empire is decided. It, of course, greatly attracted the attention of mankind, and has since taken its place among the most renowned combats of history.

Pultowa is a town situated in the heart of the Russian territories three or four hundred miles north of the Black Sea. It stands on a small river which flows to the southward and westward into the Dnieper. It was at that time an important military station, as it contained great arsenals where large stores of food and of ammunition were laid up for the use of Peter's army. The King of Sweden determined to take this town. His principal object in desiring to get possession of it was to supply the wants of his army by the provisions that were stored there. The place was strongly fortified, and it was defended by a garrison; but the king thought that he should be able to take it, and he accordingly advanced to the walls, invested the place closely on every side, and commenced the siege.

The name of the general in command of the largest body of Russian forces near the spot was Menzikoff, and as soon as the King of Sweden had invested the place, Menzikoff began to advance toward it in order to relieve it. Then followed a long series of manoeuvres and partial combats between the two armies, the Swedes being occupied with the double duty of attacking the town, and also of defending themselves from Menzikoff; while Menzikoff, on the other hand, was intent, first on harassing the Swedes and impeding as much as possible their siege operations, and, secondly, on throwing succors into the town.

In this contest Menzikoff was, on the whole, most successful. He contrived one night to pass a detachment of his troops through the gates of Pultowa into the town to strengthen the garrison. This irritated the King of Sweden, and made him more determined and reckless than ever to press the siege. Under this excitement he advanced so near the walls one day, in a desperate effort to take possession of an advanced part of the works, that he exposed himself to a shot from the ramparts, and was badly wounded in the heel.

This wound nearly disabled him. He was obliged by it to confine himself to his tent, and to content himself with giving orders from his couch or litter, where he lay helpless and in great pain, and in a state of extreme mental disquietude.

His anxiety was greatly increased in a few days in consequence of intelligence which was brought into his camp by the scouts, that Peter himself was advancing to the relief of Pultowa at the head of a very large army. Indeed, the tidings were that this great force was close at hand. The king found that he was in danger of being surrounded. Nor could he well hope to escape the danger by a retreat, for the broad and deep river Dnieper, which he had crossed to come to the siege of Pultowa, was behind him, and if the Russians were to fall upon him while attempting to cross it, he knew very well that his whole army would be cut to pieces.

He lay restless on his litter in his tent, his thoughts divided between the anguish of the wound in his heel and the mental anxiety and distress produced by the situation that he was in. He spent the night in great perplexity and suffering. At length, toward morning, he came to the desperate resolution of attacking the Russians in their camp, inferior as his own numbers were now to theirs.

He accordingly sent a messenger to the field-marshal, who was chief officer in command under himself, summoning him to his tent. The field-marshal was aroused from his sleep, for it was not yet day, and immediately repaired to the king's tent. The king was lying on his couch, quiet and calm, and, with an air of great serenity and composure, he gave the marshal orders to beat to arms and march out to attack the Czar in his intrenchments as soon as daylight should appear.

The field-marshal was astonished at this order, for he knew that the Russians were now far superior in numbers to the Swedes, and he supposed that the only hope of the king would be to defend himself where he was in his camp, or else to attempt a retreat. He, however, knew that there was nothing to be done but to obey his orders. So he received the instructions which the king gave him, said that he would carry them into execution, and then retired. The king then at length fell into a troubled sleep, and slept until the break of day.

By this time the whole camp was in motion. The Russians, too, who in their intrenchments had received the alarm, had aroused themselves and were preparing for battle. The Czar himself was not the commander. He had prided himself, as the reader will recollect, in entering the army at the lowest point, and in advancing regularly, step by step, through all the grades, as any other officer would have done. He had now attained the rank of major general; and though, as Czar, he gave orders through his ministers to the commander-in-chief of the armies directing them in general what to do, still personally, in camp and in the field of battle, he received orders from his military superior there; and he took a pride and pleasure in the subordination to his superior's authority which the rules of the service required of him.

He, however, as it seems, did not always entirely lay aside his imperial character while in camp, for in this instance, while the men were formed in array, and before the battle commenced, he rode to and fro along their lines, encouraging the men, and promising, as their sovereign, to bestow rewards upon them in proportion to the valor which they should severally display in the coming combat.

The King of Sweden, too, was raised from his couch, placed upon a litter, and in this manner carried along the lines of his own army just before the battle was to begin. He told the men that they were about to attack an enemy more numerous than themselves, but that they must remember that at Narva eight thousand Swedes had overcome a hundred thousand Russians in their own intrenchments, and what they had done once, he said, they could do again.

The battle was commenced very early in the morning. It was complicated at the beginning with many marches, counter-marches, and manoeuvres, in which the several divisions of both the Russian and Swedish armies, and the garrison of Pultowa, all took part. In some places and at some times the victory was on one side, and at others on the other. King Charles was carried in his litter into the thickest of the battle, where, after a time, he became so excited by the contest that he insisted on being put upon a horse. The attendants accordingly brought a horse and placed him carefully upon it; but the pain of his wound brought on faintness, and he was obliged to be put back in his litter again. Soon after this a cannon ball struck the litter and dashed it to pieces. The king was thrown out upon the ground. Those who saw him fall supposed that he was killed, and they were struck with consternation. They had been almost overpowered by their enemies before, but they were now wholly disheartened and discouraged, and they began to give way and fly in all directions.

The king had, however, not been touched by the ball which struck the litter. He was at once raised from the ground by

Jacob Abbott

the officers around him, and borne away out of the immediate danger. He remonstrated earnestly against being taken away, and insisted upon making an effort to rally his men; but the officers soon persuaded him that for the present, at least, all was lost, and that the only hope for him was to make his escape as soon as possible across the river, and thence over the frontier into Turkey, where he would be safe from pursuit, and could then consider what it would be best to do.

The king at length reluctantly yielded to these persuasions, and was borne away.

In the mean time, the Czar himself had been exposed to great danger in the battle, and, like the King of Sweden, had met with some very narrow escapes. His hat was shot through with a bullet which half an inch lower would have gone through the emperor's head. General Menzikoff had three horses shot under him. But, notwithstanding these dangers, the Czar pressed on into the thickest of the fight, and was present at the head of his men when the Swedes were finally overwhelmed and driven from the field. Indeed, he was among the foremost who pursued them; and when he came to the place where the royal litter was lying, broken to pieces, on the ground, he expressed great concern for the fate of his enemy, and seemed to regret the calamity which had befallen him as if Charles had been his friend. He had always greatly admired the courage and the military skill which the King of Sweden had manifested in his campaigns, and was disposed to respect his misfortunes now that he had fallen. He supposed that he was unquestionably killed, and he gave orders to his men to search every where over the field for the body, and to guard it, when found, from any farther violence or injury, and take charge of it, that it might receive an honorable burial.

The body was, of course, not found, for the king was alive, and, with the exception of the wound in his heel, uninjured. He was borne off from the field by a few faithful adherents, who took him in their arms when the litter was broken up. As soon as they had conveyed him in this manner out of immediate danger, they hastily constructed another litter in order to bear him farther away. He was himself extremely unwilling to go. He was very earnest to make an effort to rally his men, and, if possible, save his army from total ruin. But he soon found that it was in vain to attempt this. His whole force had been thrown into utter confusion; and the broken battalions, flying in every direction, were pursued so hotly by the Russians, who, in their exultant fury, slaughtered all whom they could overtake, and drove the rest headlong on in a state of panic and dismay which was wholly uncontrollable.

Of course some escaped, but great numbers were taken prisoners. Many of the officers, separated from their men, wandered about in search of the king, being without any rallying point until they could find him. After suffering many cruel hardships and much exposure in the lurking-places where they attempted to conceal themselves, great numbers of them were hunted out by their enemies and made prisoners.

In the mean time, those who had the king under their charge urged his majesty to allow them to convey him with all speed out of the country. The nearest way of escape was to go westward to the Turkish frontier, which, as has already been said, was not far distant, though there were three rivers to cross on the way—the Dnieper, the Bog, and the Dniester. The king was very unwilling to listen to this advice. Peter had several times sent a flag of truce to him since he had entered into the Russian dominions, expressing a desire to make peace, and proposing very reasonable terms for

Charles to accede to. To all these proposals Charles had returned the same answer as at first, which was, that he should not be ready to treat with the Czar until he arrived at Moscow. Charles now said that, before abandoning the country altogether, he would send a herald to the Russian camp to say that he was now willing to make peace on the terms which Peter had before proposed to him, if Peter was still willing to adhere to them.

Charles was led to hope that this proposal might perhaps be successful, from the fact that there was a portion of his army who had not been engaged at Pultowa that was still safe; and he had no doubt that a very considerable number of men would succeed in escaping from Pultowa and joining them. Indeed, the number was not small of those whom the king had now immediately around him, for all that escaped from the battle made every possible exertion to discover and rejoin the king, and so many straggling parties came that he soon had under his command a force of one or two thousand men. This was, of course, but a small remnant of his army. Still, he felt that he was not wholly destitute of means and resources for carrying on the struggle in case Peter should refuse to make peace.

So he sent a trumpeter to Peter's camp with the message; but Peter sent word back that his majesty's assent to the terms of peace which he had proposed to him came too late. The state of things had now, he said, entirely changed; and as Charles had ventured to penetrate into the Russian country without properly considering the consequences of his rashness, he must now think for himself how he was to get out of it. For his part, he added, he had got the birds in the net, and he should do all in his power to secure them.

After due consultation among the officers who were with the king, it was finally determined that it was useless to think for the present of any farther resistance, and the king, at last, reluctantly consented to be conveyed to the Turkish frontier. He was too ill from the effects of his wound to ride on horseback, and the distance was too great for him to be conveyed in a litter. So they prepared a carriage for him. It was a carriage which belonged to one of his generals, and which, by some means or other, had been saved in the flight of the army. The route which they were to take led across the country where there were scarcely any roads, and a team of twelve horses was harnessed to draw the carriage which conveyed the king.

No time was to be lost. The confused mass of officers and men who had escaped from the battle, and had succeeded in rejoining the king, were marshaled into something like a military organization, and the march, or rather the flight, commenced. The king's carriage, attended by such a guard as could be provided for it, went before, and was followed by the remnant of the army. Some of the men were on horseback, others were on foot, and others still, sick or wounded, were conveyed on little wagons of the country, which were drawn along in a very difficult and laborious manner.

This mournful train moved slowly on across the country, seeking, of course, the most retired and solitary ways to avoid pursuit, and yet harassed by the continual fear that the enemy might at any time come up with them. The men all suffered exceedingly from want of food, and from the various other hardships incident to their condition. Many became so worn out by fatigue and privation that they could not proceed, and were left by the road sides to fall into the hands of the enemy, or to perish of want and exhaustion; while those who still had strength enough remaining pressed despairingly onward, but little less to be pitied than those who were left behind.

Jacob Abbott

When at length the expedition drew near to the Turkish borders, the king sent forward a messenger to the pasha in command on the frontier, asking permission for himself and his men to pass through the Turkish territory on his way to his own dominions. He had every reason to suppose that the pasha would grant this request, for the Turks and Russians had long been enemies, and he knew very well that the sympathies of the Turks had been entirely on his side in this war.

Nor was he disappointed in his expectations. The pasha received the messenger very kindly, offered him food, and supplied all his wants. He said, moreover, that he would not only give the king leave to enter and pass through the Turkish territories, but he would give him efficient assistance in crossing the river which formed the frontier. This was, indeed, necessary, for a large detachment of the Russian army which had been sent in pursuit of the Swedes was now coming close upon them, and there was danger of their being overtaken and cut to pieces or taken prisoners before they should have time to cross the stream. The principal object which the Czar had in view in sending a detachment in pursuit of the fugitives was the hope of capturing the king himself. He spoke of this his design to the Swedish officers who were already his prisoners, saying to them jocosely, for he was in excellent humor with every body after the battle, "I have a great desire to see my brother the king, and to enjoy his society; so I have sent to bring him. You will see him here in a few days."

The force dispatched for this purpose had been gradually gaining upon the fugitives, and was now very near, and the pasha, on learning the facts, perceived that the exigency was very urgent. He accordingly sent off at once up and down the river to order all the boats that could be found to repair immediately to the spot where the King of Sweden wished to cross. A considerable number of boats were soon collected, and the passage was immediately commenced. The king and his guards were brought over safely, and also a large number of the officers and men. But the boats were, after all, so few that the operation proceeded slowly, and the Russians, who had been pressing on with all speed, arrived at the banks of the river in time to interrupt it before all the troops had passed, and thus about five hundred men fell into their hands. They were all made prisoners, and the king had the mortification of witnessing the spectacle of their capture from the opposite bank, which he had himself reached in safety.

The king was immediately afterward conveyed to Bender, a considerable town not far from the frontier, where, for the present, he was safe, and where he remained quiet for some weeks, in order that his wound might have opportunity to heal. Peter was obliged to content himself with postponing for a time the pleasure which he expected to derive from the enjoyment of his brother's society.

The portion of the Swedish army which remained in Russia was soon after this surrounded by so large a Russian force that the general in command was forced to capitulate, and all the troops were surrendered as prisoners of war. Thus, in all, a great number of prisoners, both of officers and men, fell into Peter's hands. The men were sent to various parts of the empire, and distributed among the people, in order that they might settle permanently in the country, and devote themselves to the trades or occupations to which they had been trained in their native land. The officers were treated with great kindness and consideration. Peter often invited them to his table, and conversed with them in a very free and friendly manner in respect to the usages and customs which prevailed in their own country, especially those which related to the military art. Still, they were deprived of their swords and kept close prisoners.

One day, when some of these officers were dining with Peter in his tent, and he had been for some time conversing with them about the organization and discipline of the Swedish army, and had expressed great admiration for the military talent and skill which they had displayed in the campaigns which they had fought, he at last poured out some wine and drank to the health of "his masters in the art of war." One of the officers who was present asked who they were that his majesty was pleased to honor with so great a title.

"It is yourselves, gentlemen," replied the Czar; "the Swedish generals. It is you who have been my best instructors in the art of war."

"Then," replied the officer, "is not your majesty a little ungrateful to treat the masters to whom you owe so much so severely?"

Peter was so much pleased with the readiness and wit of this reply, that he ordered the swords of the officers all to be restored to them. It is said that he even unbuckled his own sword from his side and presented it to one of the generals.

It ought, perhaps, to be added, however, that the habit of drinking to excess, which Peter seems to have formed early in life, had before this time become quite confirmed, and he often became completely intoxicated at his convivial entertainments, so that it is not improbable that the sudden generosity of the Czar on this occasion may have been due, in a considerable degree, to the excitement produced by the brandy which he had been drinking.

Although the swords of the officers were thus restored to them, they were themselves still held as prisoners until arrangements could be made for exchanging them. In order, however, that they might all be properly provided for, he distributed them around among his own generals, giving to each Russian officer the charge of a Swedish officer of his own rank, granting, of course, to each one a proper allowance for the maintenance and support of his charge. The Russian generals were severally responsible for the safe-keeping of their prisoners; but the surveillance in such cases is never strict, for it is customary for the prisoners to give their *parole* of honor that they will not attempt to escape, and then they are allowed, within reasonable limits, their full personal liberty, so that they live more like the guests and companions of their keepers than as their captives.

The King of Sweden met with many remarkable adventures and encountered very serious difficulties before he reached his own kingdom, but it would be foreign to the subject of this history to relate them here. As to Mazeppa, he made his escape too, with the King of Sweden, across the frontier. The Czar offered a very large reward to whoever should bring him back, either dead or alive; but he never was taken. He died afterward at Constantinople at a great age.

One of the most curious and characteristic results which followed from the battle of Pultowa was the promotion of Peter in respect to his rank in the army. It was gravely decided by the proper authorities, after due deliberation, that in consequence of the vigor and bravery which he had displayed on the field, and of the danger which he had incurred in having had a shot through his hat, he deserved to be advanced a grade in the line of promotion. So he was made a major general.

Thus ended the great Swedish invasion of Russia, which was the occasion of the greatest and, indeed, of almost the only serious danger, from any foreign source, which threatened the dominions of Peter during the whole course of his reign.

CHAPTER XIV

THE EMPRESS CATHARINE

1709-1715

Duration of the war with Sweden—Catharine—Her origin—
Destitution—Her kind teacher—Dr. Gluck—She goes to
Marienburg—Her character—Mode of life at Marienburg—
Her lover—His person and character—Catharine is
married—The town captured—Catharine made prisoner—
Her anxiety and sorrow—The Russian general—Catharine
saved—Catharine in the general's service—Seen by
Menzikoff—Transferred to his service—Transferred to the
Czar—Privately married—Affairs on the Pruth—The
emperor's danger—Catharine in camp—A bribe—Catharine
saves her husband—The vizier's excuses—A public marriage
determined on—Arrangements—The little bridesmaids—
Wedding ceremonies—Festivities and rejoicings—Birth of
Catharine's son—Importance of the event—The baptism—
Dwarfs in the pies—Influence of Catharine over her
husband—Use which she made of her power—Peter's
jealousy—Dreadful punishment—Catharine's usefulness to
the Czar—Her imperfect education—Her final exaltation to
the throne

It was about the year 1690 that Peter the Great commenced

his reign, and he died in 1725, as will appear more fully in the sequel of this volume. Thus the duration of the reign was thirty-five years. The wars between Russia and Sweden occupied principally the early part of the reign through a period of many years. The battle of Pultowa, by which the Swedish invasion of the Russian territories was repelled, was fought in 1709, nearly twenty years after the Czar ascended the throne.

During the period while the Czar was thus occupied in his mortal struggle with the King of Sweden, there appeared upon the stage, in connection with him, a lady, who afterward became one of the most celebrated personages of history. This lady was the Empress Catharine. The character of this lady, the wonderful and romantic incidents of her life, and the great fame of her exploits, have made her one of the most celebrated personages of history. We can, however, here only give a brief account of that portion of her life which was connected with the history of Peter.

Catharine was born in a little village near the town of Marienburg, in Livonia.[1] Her parents were in very humble circumstances, and they both died when she was a little child, leaving her in a very destitute and friendless condition. The parish clerk, who was the teacher of a little school in which perhaps she had been a pupil—for she was then four or five years old—felt compassion for her, and took her home with him to his own house. He was the more disposed to do this as Catharine was a bright child, full of life and activity, and, at the same time, amiable and docile in disposition, so that she was easily governed.

After Catharine had been some time at the house of the clerk, a certain Dr. Gluck, who was the minister of Marienburg, happening to be on a visit to the clerk, saw her and heard her story. The minister was very much pleased with the

Jacob Abbott

appearance and manners of the child, and he proposed that the clerk should give her up to him. This the clerk was willing to do, as his income was very small, and the addition even of such a child to his family of course somewhat increased his expenses. Besides, he knew that it would be much more advantageous for Catharine, for the time being, and also much more conducive to her future success in life, to be brought up in the minister's family at Marienburg than in his own humble home in the little village. So Catharine went to live with the minister.[2]

Here she soon made herself a great favorite. She was very intelligent and active, and very ambitious to learn whatever the minister's wife was willing to teach her. She also took great interest in making herself useful in every possible way, and displayed in her household avocations, and in all her other duties, a sort of womanly energy which was quite remarkable in one of her years. She learned to knit, to spin, and to sew, and she assisted the minister's wife very much in these and similar occupations. She had learned to read in her native tongue at the clerk's school, but now she conceived the idea of learning the German language. She devoted herself to this task with great assiduity and success, and as soon as she had made such progress as to be able to read in that language, she spent all her leisure time in perusing the German books which she found in the minister's library.

Years passed away, and Catharine grew up to be a young woman, and then a certain young man, a subaltern officer in the Swedish army—for this was at the time when Livonia was ill possession of the Swedes—fell in love with her. The story was, that Catharine one day, in some way or other, fell into the hands of two Swedish soldiers, by whom she would probably have been greatly maltreated; but the officer, coming by at that time, rescued her and sent her safe to Dr. Gluck. The officer had lost one of his arms in some battle, and was covered with the scars of other wounds; but he was a very generous and brave man, and was highly regarded by all who knew him. When he offered Catharine his hand, she was strongly induced by her gratitude to him to accept it, but she said she must ask the minister's approval of his proposal, for he had been a father to her, she said, and she would take no important step without his consent.

The minister, after suitable inquiry respecting the officer's character and prospects, readily gave his consent, and so it was settled that Catharine should be married.

Now it happened that these occurrences took place not very long after the war broke out between Sweden and Russia, and almost immediately after Catharine's marriage—some writers say on the very same day of the wedding, and others on the day following—a Russian army came suddenly up to Marienburg, took possession of the town, and made a great many of the inhabitants prisoners. Catharine herself was among the prisoners thus taken. The story was, that in the confusion and alarm she hid herself with others in an oven, and was found by the Russian soldiers there, and carried off as a valuable prize.

What became of the bridegroom is not certainly known. He was doubtless called suddenly to his post when the alarm was given of the enemy's approach, and a great many different stories were told in respect to what afterward befell him. One thing is certain, and that is, that his young bride never saw him again.[3]

Catharine, when she found herself separated from her husband and shut up a helpless prisoner with a crowd of other wretched and despairing captives, was overwhelmed with grief at the sad reverse of fortune that had befallen her. She had good reason not only to mourn for the happiness

Jacob Abbott

which she had lost, but also to experience very anxious and gloomy forebodings in respect to what was before her, for the main object of the Russians in making prisoners of the young and beautiful women which they found in the towns that they conquered, was to send them to Turkey, and to sell them there as slaves.

Catharine was, however, destined to escape this dreadful fate. One of the Russian generals, in looking over the prisoners, was struck with her appearance, and with the singular expression of grief and despair which her countenance displayed. He called her to him and asked her some questions; and he was more impressed by the intelligence and good sense which her answers evinced than he had been by the beauty of her countenance. He bid her quiet her fears, promising that he would himself take care of her. He immediately ordered some trusty men to take her to his tent, where there were some women who would take charge of and protect her.

These women were employed in various domestic occupations in the service of the general. Catharine began at once to interest herself in these employments, and to do all in her power to assist in them; and at length, as one of the writers who gives an account of these transactions goes on to say, "the general, finding Catharine very proper to manage his household affairs, gave her a sort of authority and inspection over these women and over the rest of the domestics, by whom she soon came to be very much beloved by her manner of using them when she instructed them in their duty. The general said himself that he never had been so well served as since Catharine had been with him.

"It happened one day that Prince Menzikoff, who was the general's commanding officer and patron, saw Catharine, and, observing something very extraordinary in her air and behavior, asked the general who she was and in what condition she served him. The general related to him her story, taking care, at the same time, to do justice to the merit of Catharine. The prince said that he was himself very ill served, and had occasion for just such a person about him. The general replied that he was under too great obligations to his highness the prince to refuse him any thing that he asked. He immediately called Catharine into his presence, and told her that that was Prince Menzikoff, and that he had occasion for a servant like herself, and that he was able to be a much better friend to her than he himself could be, and that he had too much kindness for her to prevent her receiving such a piece of honor and good fortune.

"Catharine answered only with a profound courtesy, which showed, if not her consent to the change proposed, at least her conviction that it was not then in her power to refuse the offer that was made to her. In short, Prince Menzikoff took her with him, or she went to him the same day."

Catharine remained in the service of the prince for a year or two, and was then transferred from the household of the prince to that of the Czar almost precisely in the same way in which she had been resigned to the prince by the general. The Czar saw her one day while he was at dinner with the prince, and he was so much pleased with her appearance, and with the account which the prince gave him of her character and history, that he wished to have her himself; and, however reluctant the prince may have been to lose her, he knew very well that there was no alternative for him but to give his consent. So Catharine was transferred to the household of the Czar.

She soon acquired a great ascendency over the Czar, and in process of time she was privately married to him. This private marriage took place in 1707. For several years afterward the marriage was not publicly acknowledged; but still Catharine's position was well understood, and her power at court, as well as her personal influence over her husband, increased continually.

Catharine sometimes accompanied the emperor in his military campaigns, and at one time was the means, it is thought, of saving him from very imminent danger. It was in the year 1711. The Czar was at that time at war with the Turks, and he had advanced into the Turkish territory with a small, but very compact and well-organized army. The Turks sent out a large force to meet him, and at length, after various marchings and manoeuvrings, the Czar found himself surrounded by a Turkish force three times as large as his own. The Russians fortified their camp, and the Turks attacked them. The latter attempted for two or three successive days to force the Russian lines, but without success, and at length the grand vizier, who was in command of the Turkish troops, finding that he could not force his enemy to quit their intrenchments, determined to starve them out; so he invested the place closely on all sides. The Czar now gave himself up for lost, for he had only a very small stock of provisions, and there seemed no possible way of escape from the snare in which he found himself involved. Catharine was with her husband in the camp at this time, having had the courage to accompany him in the expedition, notwithstanding its extremely dangerous character, and the story is that she was the means of extricating him from his hazardous position by dextrously bribing the vizier.

The way in which she managed the affair was this. She arranged it with the emperor that he was to propose terms of peace to the vizier, by which, on certain conditions, he was to be allowed to retire with his army. Catharine then secretly made up a very valuable present for the vizier, consisting of jewels, costly decorations, and other such valuables belonging to herself, which, as was customary in those times, she had brought with her on the expedition, and also a large sum of money. This present she contrived to send to the vizier at the same time with the proposals of peace made by the emperor. The vizier was extremely pleased with the present, and he at once agreed to the conditions of peace, and thus the Czar and all his army escaped the destruction which threatened them.

The vizier was afterward called to account for having thus let off his enemies so easily when he had them so completely in his power; but he defended himself as well as he could by saying that the terms on which he had made the treaty were as good as could be obtained in any way, adding, hypocritically, that "God commands us to pardon our enemies when they ask us to do so, and humble themselves before us."

In the mean time, years passed away, and the emperor and Catharine lived very happily together, though the connection which subsisted between them, while it was universally known, was not openly or publicly recognized. In process of time they had two or three children, and this, together with the unassuming but yet faithful and efficient manner in which Catharine devoted herself to her duties as wife and mother, strengthened the bond which bound her to the Czar, and at length, in the year 1712, Peter determined to place her before the world in the position to which he had already privately and unofficially raised her, by a new and public marriage.

It was not pretended, however, that the Czar was to be married to Catharine now for the first time, but the celebration was to be in honor of the nuptials long before performed. Accordingly, in the invitations that were sent out, the expression used to denote the occasion on which the company was to be convened was "to celebrate his majesty's old wedding." The place where the ceremony was to be performed was St. Petersburg, for this was now many years after St. Petersburg had been built.

Very curious arrangements were made for the performance of this extraordinary ceremony. The Czar appeared in the dress and character of an admiral of the fleet, and the other officers of the fleet, instead of the ministers of state and great nobility, were made most prominent on the occasion, and were appointed to the most honorable posts. This arrangement was made partly, no doubt, for the purpose of doing honor to the navy, which the Czar was now forming, and increasing the consideration of those who were connected with it in the eyes of the country. As Catharine had no parents living, it was necessary to appoint persons to act in their stead "to give away the bride." It was to the vice admiral and the rear admiral of the fleet that the honor of acting in this capacity was assigned. They represented the bride's father, while Peter's mother, the empress dowager, and the lady of the vice admiral of the fleet represented her mother.

Two of Catharine's own daughters were appointed brides-maids. Their appointment was, however, not much more than an honorary one, for the children were very young, one of them being five and the other only three years old. They appeared for a little time pending the ceremony, and then, becoming tired, they were taken away, and their places supplied by two young ladies of the court, nieces of the Czar.

The wedding ceremony itself was performed at seven o'clock in the morning, in a little chapel belonging to Prince Menzikoff, and before a small company, no person being present at that time except those who had some official part to perform. The great wedding party had been invited to meet at the Czar's palace later in the day. After the ceremony had been performed in the chapel, the emperor and empress went from the chapel into Menzikoff's palace, and remained there until the time arrived to repair to the palace of the Czar. Then a grand procession was formed, and the married pair were conducted through the streets to their own palace with great parade. As it was winter, the bridal party were conveyed in sleighs instead of carriages. These sleighs, or sledges as they were called, were very elegantly decorated, and were drawn by six horses each. The procession was accompanied by a band of music, consisting of trumpets, kettle-drums, and other martial instruments. The entertainment at the palace was very splendid, and the festivities were concluded in the evening by a ball. The whole city, too, was lighted up that night with bonfires and illuminations.

Three years after this public solemnization of the marriage the empress gave birth to a son. Peter was perfectly overjoyed at this event. It is true that he had one son already, who was born of his first wife, who was called the Czarewitz, and whose character and melancholy history will be the subject of the next chapter. But this was the first son among the children of Catharine. She had had only daughters before. It was in the very crisis of the difficulties which the Czar had with his eldest son, and when he was on the point of finally abandoning all hope of ever reclaiming him from his vices and making him a fit inheritor of the crown, that this child of Catharine's was born. These circumstances, which will be explained more fully in the next chapter, gave great political importance to the birth of Catharine's son, and Peter caused the event to be celebrated with great public rejoicings. The rejoicings were continued for eight days, and at the baptism of the babe, two kings, those of Denmark and of Prussia, acted as godfathers. The name given to the child was Peter Petrowitz.

Jacob Abbott

The baptism was celebrated with the greatest pomp, and it was attended with banquetings and rejoicings of the most extraordinary character. Among other curious contrivances were two enormous pies, one served in the room of the gentlemen and the other in that of the ladies; for, according to the ancient Russian custom on such occasions, the sexes were separated at the entertainments, tables being spread for the ladies and for the gentlemen in different halls. From the ladies' pie there stepped out, when it was opened, a young dwarf, very small, and clothed in a very slight and very fantastic manner. The dwarf brought out with him from the pie some wine-glasses and a bottle of wine. Taking these in his hand, he walked around the table drinking to the health of the ladies, who received him wherever he came with screams of mingled surprise and laughter. It was the same in the gentlemen's apartment, except that the dwarf which appeared before the company there was a female.

The birth of this son formed a new and very strong bond of attachment between Peter and Catharine, and it increased very much the influence which she had previously exerted over him. The influence which she thus exercised was very great, and it was also, in the main, very salutary. She alone could approach the Czar in the fits of irritation and anger into which he often fell when any thing displeased him, and sometimes, when his rage and fury were such, that no one else would have dared to come near, Catharine knew how to quiet and calm him, and gradually bring him back again to reason. She had great power over him, too, in respect to the nervous affection—the convulsive twitchings of the head and face—to which he was subject. Indeed, it was said that the soothing and mysterious influence of her gentle nursing in allaying these dreadful spasms, and relieving the royal patient from the distress which they occasioned, gave rise to the first feeling of attachment which he formed for her, and which led him, in the end, to make her his wife.

Catharine often exerted the power which she acquired over her husband for noble ends. A great many persons, who from time to time excited the displeasure of the Czar, were rescued from undeserved death, and sometimes from sufferings still more terrible than death, by her interposition. In many ways she softened the asperities of Peter's character, and lightened the heavy burden of his imperial despotism. Every one was astonished at the ascendency which she acquired over the violent and cruel temper of her husband, and equally pleased with the good use which she made of her power.

There was not, however, always perfect peace between Catharine and her lord. Catharine was compelled sometimes to endure great trials. On one occasion the Czar took it into his head, with or without cause, to feel jealous. The object of his jealousy was a certain officer of his court whose name was De la Croix. Peter had no certain evidence, it would seem, to justify his suspicions, for he said nothing openly on the subject, but he at once caused the officer to be beheaded on some other pretext, and ordered his head to be set up on a pole in a great public square in Moscow. He then took Catharine out into the square, and conveyed her to and fro in all directions across it, in order that she might see the head in every point of view. Catharine understood perfectly well what it all meant, but, though thunderstruck and overwhelmed with grief and horror at the terrible spectacle, she succeeded in maintaining a perfect self-control through the whole scene, until, at length, she was released, and allowed to return to her apartment, when she burst into tears, and for a long time could not be comforted or calmed.

With the exception of an occasional outbreak like this, the Czar evinced a very strong attachment to his consort, and she continued to live with him a faithful and devoted wife for nearly twenty years; from the period of her private marriage, in fact, to the death of her husband. During all this time she was continually associated with him not only in his personal and private, but also in his public avocations and cares. She accompanied him on his journeys, she aided him with her counsels in all affairs of state. He relied a great deal on her judgment in all questions of policy, whether internal or external; and he took counsel with her in all matters connected with his negotiations with foreign states, with the sending and receiving of embassies, the making of treaties with them, and even, when occasion occurred, in determining the question of peace or war.

And yet, notwithstanding the lofty qualities of statesmanship that Catharine thus displayed in the counsel and aid which she rendered her husband, the education which she had received while at the minister's in Marienburg was so imperfect that she never learned to write, and whenever, either during her husband's life or after his death, she had occasion to put her signature to letters or documents of any kind, she did not attempt to write the name herself, but always employed one of her daughters to do it for her.

At length, toward the close of his reign, Peter, having at that time no son to whom he could intrust the government of his empire after he was gone, caused Catharine to be solemnly crowned as empress, with a view of making her his successor on the throne. But before describing this coronation it is necessary first to give an account of the circumstances which led to it, by relating the melancholy history of Alexis, Peter's oldest son.

[1] The situation of the place is shown in the map on page 197.

[2] The accounts which different historians give of the circumstances of Catharine's early history vary very

materially. One authority states that the occasion of Gluck's taking Catharine away was the death of the curate and of all his family by the plague. Gluck came, it is said, to the house to see the family, and found them all dead. The bodies were lying on the floor, and little Catharine was running about among them, calling upon one after another to give her some bread. After Gluck came in, and while he was looking at the bodies in consternation, she came up behind him and pulled his robe, and asked him if he would not give her some bread. So he took her with him to his own home.

[3] There was a story that he was taken among the prisoners at the battle of Pultowa, and that, on making himself known, he was immediately put in irons and sent off in exile to Siberia.

CHAPTER XV

THE PRINCE ALEXIS

1690-1716

Birth of Alexis—His father's hopes—Advantages enjoyed by Alexis—Marriage proposed—Account of the wedding—Alexis returns to Russia—Cruel treatment of his wife—Her hardships and sufferings—The Czar's displeasure—Birth of a son—Cruel neglect—The Czar sent for—Death-bed scene—Grief of the attendants—The princess's despair—High rank no guarantee for happiness—Peter's ultimatum—Letter to Alexis—Positive declarations contained in it—The real ground of complaint—Alexis's excuses—His reply to his father—He surrenders his claim to the crown—Another letter from the Czar—New threats—More positive declarations—Alexis's answer—Real state of his health—His depraved character—The companions and counselors of Alexis—Priests—Designs of Alexis's companions—General policy of an opposition—The old Muscovite party—Views of Alexis—Peter at a loss—One more final determination—Farewell conversation—Alexis's duplicity—Letter from Copenhagen—Alternative offered—Peter's unreasonable severity—Alexis made desperate—Alexis's resolution

The reader will perhaps recollect that Peter had a son by his first wife, an account of whose birth was given in the first part of this volume. The name of this son was Alexis, and he was destined to become the hero of a most dreadful tragedy. The narrative of it forms a very dark and melancholy chapter in the history of his father's reign.

Alexis was born in the year 1690. In the early part of his life his father took great interest in him, and made him the centre of a great many ambitious hopes and projects. Of course, he expected that Alexis would be his successor on the imperial throne, and he took great interest in qualifying him for the duties that would devolve upon him in that exalted station. While he was a child his father was proud of him as his son and heir, and as he grew up he hoped that he would inherit his own ambition and energy, and he took great pains to inspire him with the lofty sentiments appropriate to his position, and to train him to a knowledge of the art of war.

But Alexis had no taste for these things, and his father could not, in any possible way, induce him to take any interest in them whatever. He was idle and spiritless, and nothing could arouse him to make any exertion. He spent his time in indolence and in vicious indulgences. These habits had the effect of undermining his health, and increasing more and more his distaste for the duties which his father wished him to perform.

The Czar tried every possible means to produce a change in the character of his son, and to awaken in him something like an honorable ambition. To this end he took Alexis with him in his journeys to foreign countries, and introduced him to the reigning princes of eastern Europe, showed him their capitals, explained to him the various military systems which were adopted by the different powers, and made him acquainted with the principal personages in their courts. But all was of no avail. Alexis could not be aroused to take an interest in any thing but idle indulgences and vice.

At length, when Alexis was about twenty years of age, that is, in the year 1710, his father conceived the idea of trying the effect of marriage upon him. So he directed his son to make choice of a wife. It is not improbable that he himself really selected the lady. At any rate, he controlled the selection, for Alexis was quite indifferent in respect to the affair, and only acceded to the plan in obedience to his father's commands.

The lady chosen for the bride was a Polish princess, named Charlotta Christina Sophia, Princess of Wolfenbuttel, and a marriage contract, binding the parties to each other, was executed with all due formality.

Two years after this marriage contract was formed the marriage was celebrated. Alexis was then about twenty-two years of age, and the princess eighteen. The wedding, however, was by no means a joyful one. Alexis had not improved in character since he had been betrothed, and his father continued to be very much displeased with him. Peter was at one time so angry as to threaten that, if his son did not reform his evil habits, and begin to show some interest in the performance of his duties, he would have his head shaved and send him to a convent, and so make a monk of him.

How far the princess herself was acquainted with the facts in respect to the character of her husband it is impossible to say, but every body else knew them very well. The emperor was in very bad humor. The princess's father wished to arrange for a magnificent wedding, but the Czar would not permit it. The ceremony was accordingly performed in a very quiet and unostentatious way, in one of the provincial towns of Poland, and after it was over Alexis went home with his bride to her paternal domains.

The marriage of Alexis to the Polish princess took place the year before his father's public marriage with his second wife, the Empress Catharine.

As Peter had anticipated, the promises of reform which Alexis had made on the occasion of his marriage failed totally of accomplishment. After remaining a short time in Poland with his wife, conducting himself there tolerably well, he set out on his return to Russia, taking his wife with him. But no sooner had he got back among his old associates than he returned to his evil ways, and soon began to treat his wife with the greatest neglect and even cruelty. He provided a separate suite of apartments for her in one end of the palace, while he himself occupied the other end, where he could be at liberty to do what he pleased without restraint. Sometimes a week would elapse without his seeing his wife at all. He purchased a small slave, named Afrosinia, and brought her into his part of the palace, and lived with her there in the most shameless manner, while his neglected wife, far from all her friends, alone, and almost broken-hearted, spent her time in bitterly lamenting her hard fate, and gradually wearing away her life in sorrow and tears.

She was not even properly provided with the necessary comforts of life. Her rooms were neglected, and suffered to go out of repair. The roof let in the rain, and the cold wind in the winter penetrated through the ill-fitted windows and doors. Alexis paid no heed to these things; but, leaving his wife to suffer, spent his time in drinking and carousing with Afrosinia and his other companions in vice.

During all this time the attention of the Czar was so much engaged with the affairs of the empire that he could not interfere efficiently. Sometimes he would upbraid Alexis for his undutiful and wicked behavior, and threaten him severely; but the only effect of his remonstrances would be to cause Alexis to go into the apartment of his wife as soon as his father had left him, and assail her in the most abusive manner, overwhelming her with rude and violent reproaches for having, as he said, made complaints to his father, or "told tales," as he called it, and so having occasioned his father to find fault with him. This the princess would deny. She would solemnly declare that she had not made any complaints whatever. Alexis, however, would not believe her, but would repeat his denunciations, and then go away in a rage.

This state of things continued for three or four years. During that time the princess had one child, a daughter; and at length the time arrived when she was to give birth to a son; but even the approach of such a time of trial did not awaken any feeling of kind regard or compassion on the part of her husband. His neglect still continued. No suitable arrangements were made for the princess, and she received no proper attention during her confinement. The consequence was, that, in a few days after the birth of the child, fever set in, and the princess sank so rapidly under it that her life was soon despaired of.

When she found that she was about to die, she asked that the Czar might be sent for to come and see her. Peter was sick at this time, and almost confined to his bed; but still—let it be remembered to his honor—he would not refuse this request. A bed, or litter, was placed for him on a sort of truck, and in this manner he was conveyed to the palace where the princess was lying. She thanked him very earnestly for coming to see her, and then begged to commit her children, and the servants who had come with her from her native land, and who had remained faithful to her through all her trials, to his protection and care. She kissed her children, and took leave of them in the most affecting manner, and then placed them in the arms of the Czar. The Czar received them very kindly. He then bade the mother farewell, and went away, taking the children with him.

All this time, the room in which the princess was lying, the antechamber, and all the approaches to the apartment, were filled with the servants and friends of the princess, who mourned her unhappy fate so deeply that they were unable to control their grief. They kneeled or lay prostrate on the ground, and offered unceasing petitions to heaven to save the life of their mistress, mingling their prayers with tears, and sobs, and bitter lamentations.

The physicians endeavored to persuade the princess to take some medicines which they had brought, but she threw the phials away behind the bed, begging the physicians not to torment her any more, but to let her die in peace, as she had no wish to live.

She lingered after this a few days, spending most of her time in prayer, and then died.

At the time of her death the princess was not much over twenty years of age. Her sad and sorrowful fate shows us once more what unfortunately we too often see exemplified, that something besides high worldly position in a husband is necessary to enable the bride to look forward with any degree of confidence to her prospects of happiness when receiving the congratulations of her friends on her wedding-day.

The death of his wife produced no good effect upon the mind of Alexis. At the funeral, the Czar his father addressed him in a very stern and severe manner in respect to his evil ways, and declared to him positively that, if he did not at once reform and thenceforth lead a life more in conformity with his position and his obligations, he would cut him off from the inheritance to the crown, even if it should be necessary, on that account, to call in some stranger to be his heir.

The communication which the Czar made to his son on this occasion was in writing, and the terms in which it was expressed were very severe. It commenced by reciting at length the long and fruitless efforts which the Czar had made to awaken something like an honorable ambition in the mind of his son, and to lead him to reform his habits, and concluded, substantially, as follows:

"How often have I reproached you with the obstinacy of your temper and the perverseness of your disposition! How often, even, have I corrected you for them! And now, for how many years have I desisted from speaking any longer of them! But all has been to no purpose. My reproofs have been fruitless. I have only lost my time and beaten the air. You do not so much as strive to grow better, and all your satisfaction seems to consist in laziness and inactivity.

"Having, therefore, considered all these things, and fully reflected upon them, as I see I have not been able to engage you by any motives to do as you ought, I have come to the conclusion to lay before you, in writing, this my last determination, resolving, however, to wait still a little longer before I come to a final execution of my purpose, in order to give you one more trial to see whether you will amend or no. If you do not, I am fully resolved to cut you off from the succession.

"Do not think that because I have no other son I will not really do this, but only say it to frighten you. You may rely upon it that I will certainly do what I say; for, as I spare not my own life for the good of my country and the safety of my people, why should I spare you, who will not take the pains to make yourself worthy of them? I shall much prefer to transmit this trust to some worthy stranger than to an unworthy son.

"(Signed with his majesty's own hand),

"PETER."

The reader will observe, from the phraseology of these concluding paragraphs, what is made still more evident by the perusal of the whole letter, that the great ground of Peter's complaint against his son was not his immorality and wickedness, but his idleness and inefficiency. If he had shown himself an active and spirited young man, full of military ardor, and of ambition to rule, he might probably, in his private life, have been as vicious and depraved as he pleased without exciting his father's displeasure. But Peter was himself so full of ambition and energy, and he had formed, moreover, such vast plans for the aggrandizement of the empire, many of which could only be commenced during his lifetime, and must depend for their full accomplishment on the vigor and talent of his successor, that he had set his heart very strongly on making his son one of the first military men of the age; and he now lost all patience with him when he saw him stupidly neglecting the glorious opportunity before him, and throwing away all his advantages, in order to spend his time in ease and indulgence, thus thwarting and threatening to render abortive some of his father's favorite and most far-reaching plans.

The excuse which Alexis made for his conduct was the same which bad boys often offer for idleness and delinquency, namely, his ill health. His answer to his father's letter was as follows. It was not written until two or three weeks after his father's letter was received, and in that interim a son was born to the Empress Catharine, as related in the last chapter. It is to this infant son that Alexis alludes in his letter:

"MY CLEMENT LORD AND FATHER,—

"I have read the writing your majesty gave me on the 27th of October, 1715, after the interment of my late spouse.

"I have nothing to reply to it but that if it is your majesty's pleasure to deprive me of the crown of Russia by reason of my inability—your will be done. I even earnestly request it at your majesty's hands, as I do not think myself fit for the government. My memory is much weakened, and without it there is no possibility of managing affairs. My mind and body are much decayed by the distempers to which I have been subject, which renders me incapable of governing so many people, who must necessarily require a more vigorous man at their head than I am.

"For which reason I should not aspire to the succession of the crown of Russia after you—whom God long preserve—even though I had no brother, as I have at present, whom I pray God also to preserve. Nor will I ever hereafter lay claim to the succession, as I call God to witness by a solemn oath, in confirmation whereof I write and sign this letter with my own hand.

"I give my children into your hands, and, for my part, desire no more than a bare maintenance so long as I live, leaving all the rest to your consideration and good pleasure.

"Your most humble servant and son,

    "ALEXIS."

The Czar did not immediately make any rejoinder to the foregoing communication from his son. During the fall and winter months of that year he was much occupied with public affairs, and his health, moreover, was quite infirm. At length, however, about the middle of June, he wrote to his son as follows:

"MY SON,—As my illness hath hitherto prevented me from letting you know the resolutions I have taken with reference to the answer you returned to my former letter, I now send you my reply. I observe that you there speak of the succession as though I had need of your consent to do in that respect what absolutely depends on my own will. But whence comes it that you make no mention of your voluntary indolence and inefficiency, and the aversion you constantly express to public affairs, which I spoke of in a more particular manner than of your ill health, though the latter is the only thing you take notice of? I also expressed my dissatisfaction with your whole conduct and mode of life for some years past. But of this you are wholly silent, though I strongly insisted upon it.

"From these things I judge that my fatherly exhortations make no impression upon you. For this reason I have determined to write this letter to you, and it shall be the last.

"I don't find that you make any acknowledgment of the obligation you owe to your father who gave you life. Have you assisted him, since you came to maturity of years, in his labors and pains? No, certainly. The world knows that you have not. On the other hand, you blame and abhor whatever of good I have been able to do at the expense of my health, for the love I have borne to my people, and for their advantage, and I have all imaginable reason to believe that you will destroy it all in case you should survive me.

"I can not let you continue in this way. Either change your conduct, and labor to make yourself worthy of the succession, or else take upon you the monastic vow. I can not rest satisfied with your present behavior, especially as I find that my health is declining. As soon, therefore, as you shall have received this my letter, let me have your answer in writing, or give it to me yourself in person. If you do not, I shall at once proceed against you as a malefactor.—(Signed) PETER."

To this communication Alexis the next day returned the following reply:

"MOST CLEMENT LORD AND FATHER,—

"I received yesterday in the morning your letter of the 19th of this month. My indisposition will not allow me to write a long answer. I shall enter upon a monastic life, and beg your gracious consent for so doing.

"Your most humble servant and son,

    "ALEXIS."

There is no doubt that there was some good ground for the complaints which Alexis made with respect to his health. His original constitution was not vigorous, and he had greatly impaired both his mental and physical powers by his vicious indulgences. Still, his excusing himself so much on this ground was chiefly a pretense, his object being to gain time, and prevent his father from coming to any positive decision, in order that he might continue his life of indolence and vice a little longer undisturbed. Indeed, it was said that the incapacity to attend to the studies and perform the duties which his father required of him was mainly due to his continual drunkenness, which kept him all the time in a sort of brutal stupor.

Nor was the fault wholly on his side. His father was very harsh and severe in his treatment of him, and perhaps, in the beginning, made too little allowance for the feebleness of his constitution. Neither of the two were sincere in what they said about Alexis becoming a monk. Peter, in threatening to send him to a monastery, only meant to frighten him; and Alexis, in saying that he wished to go, intended only to circumvent his father, and save himself from being molested by him any more. He knew very well that his becoming a monk would be the last thing that his father would really desire.

Besides, Alexis was surrounded by a number of companions and advisers, most of them lewd and dissolute fellows like himself, but among them were some much more cunning and far-sighted than he, and it was under their advice that he acted in all the measures that he took, and in every thing that he said and did in the course of this quarrel with his father. Among these men were several priests, who, like the rest, though priests, were vile and dissolute men. These priests, and Alexis's other advisers, told him that he was perfectly safe in pretending to accede to his father's plan to send him to a monastery, for his father would never think of such a thing as putting the threat in execution. Besides, if he did, it would do no harm; for the vows that he would take, though so utterly irrevocable in the case of common men, would all cease to be of force in his case, in the event of his father's death, and his succeeding to the throne. And, in the mean time, he could go on, they said, taking his ease and pleasure, and living as he had always done.

Many of the persons who thus took sides with Alexis, and encouraged him in his opposition to his father, had very deep designs in so doing. They were of the party who opposed the improvements and innovations which Peter had introduced, and who had in former times made the Princess Sophia their head and rallying-point in their opposition to Peter's policy. It almost always happens thus, that when, in a monarchical country, there is a party opposed to the policy which the sovereign pursues, the disaffected persons endeavor, if possible, to find a head, or leader, in some member of the royal family itself, and if they can gain to their side the one next in succession to the crown, so much the better. To this end it is for their interest to foment a quarrel in the royal family, or, if the germ of a quarrel appears, arising from some domestic or other cause, to widen the breach as much as possible, and avail themselves of the dissension to secure the name and the influence of the prince or princess thus alienated from the king as their rallying-point and centre of action.

This was just the case in the present instance. The old Muscovite party, as it was called, that is, the party opposed to the reforms and changes which Peter had made, and to the foreign influences which he had introduced into the realm, gathered around Alexis. Some of them, it was said, began secretly to form conspiracies for deposing Peter, raising Alexis nominally to the throne, and restoring the old order of things. Peter knew all this, and the fears which these rumors excited in his mind greatly increased his anxiety in respect to the course which Alexis was pursuing and the exasperation which he felt against his son. Indeed, there was reason to believe that Alexis himself, so far as he had any political opinions, had adopted the views of the malcontents. It was natural that he should do so, for the old order of things was much better adapted to the wishes and desires of a selfish and dissolute despot, who only valued his exaltation and power for the means of unlimited indulgence in sensuality and vice which they afforded. It was this supposed bias of Alexis's mind against his father's policy of reform that Peter referred to in his letter when he spoke of Alexis's desire to thwart him in his measures and undo all that he had done.

When he received Alexis's letter informing him that he was ready to enter upon the monastic life whenever his father pleased, Peter was for a time at a loss what to do. He had no intention of taking Alexis at his word, for in threatening to make a monk of him he had only meant to frighten him. For a time, therefore, after receiving this reply, he did nothing, but only vented his anger in useless imprecations and mutterings.

Peter was engaged at this time in very important public affairs arising out of the wars in which he was engaged with some foreign nations, and important negotiations which were going on with others. Not long after receiving the short letter from Alexis last cited, he was called upon to leave Russia for a time, to make a journey into central Europe. Before he went away he called to see Alexis, in order to bid him adieu, and to state to him once more what he called his final determination.

Alexis, when he heard that his father was coming, got into his bed, and received him in that way, as if he were really quite sick.

Peter asked him what conclusion he had come to. Alexis replied, as before, that he wished to enter a monastery, and that he was ready to do so at any time. His father remonstrated with him long and earnestly against this resolution. He represented in strong terms the folly of a young man like himself, in the prime of his years, and with such prospects before him, abandoning every thing, and shutting himself up all his days to the gloomy austerities of a monastic life; and he endeavored to convince him how much better it would be for him to change his course of conduct, to enter vigorously upon the fulfillment of his duties as a son and as a prince, and prepare himself for the glorious destiny which awaited him on the Russian throne.

Finally, the Czar said that he would give him six months longer to consider of it, and then, bidding him farewell, went away.

Jacob Abbott

As soon as he was gone Alexis rose from his bed, and went away to an entertainment with some of his companions. He doubtless amused them during the carousal by relating to them what had taken place during the interview with his father, and how earnestly the Czar had argued against his doing what he had begun originally with threatening to make him do.

The Czar's business called him to Copenhagen. While there he received one or two letters from Alexis, but there was nothing in them to denote any change in his intentions, and, finally, toward the end of the summer, the Czar wrote him again in the following very severe and decided manner:

"Copenhagen, Aug. 26th, 1716.

"MY SON,—Your first letter of the 29th of June, and your next of the 30th of July, were brought to me. As in them you speak only of the condition of your health, I send you the present letter to tell you that I demanded of you your resolution upon the affair of the succession when I bade you farewell. You then answered me, in your usual manner, that you judged yourself incapable of it by reason of your infirmities, and that you should choose rather to retire into a convent. I bade you seriously consider of it again, and then send me the resolution you should take. I have expected it for these seven months, and yet have heard nothing of you concerning it. You have had time enough for consideration, and, therefore, as soon as you shall receive my letter, resolve on one side or on the other.

"If you determine to apply yourself to your duties, and qualify yourself for the succession, I wish you to leave Petersburg and to come to me here within a week, so as to be here in time to be present at the opening of the campaign; but if, on the other hand, you resolve upon the monastic life, let me know when, where, and on what day you will execute your resolution, so that my mind may be at rest, and that I may know what to expect of you. Send me back your final answer by the same courier that shall bring you my letter.

"Be particular to let me know the day when you will set out from Petersburg, if you conclude to come to me, and, if not, precisely when you will perform your vow. I again tell you that I absolutely insist that you shall determine upon something, otherwise I shall conclude that you are only seeking to gain time in order that you may spend it in your customary laziness.—PETER."

When we consider that Alexis was at this time a man nearly thirty years of age, and himself the father of a family, we can easily imagine that language like this was more adapted to exasperate him and make him worse than to win him to his duty. He was, in fact, driven to a species of desperation by it, and he so far aroused himself from his usual indolence and stupidity as to form a plan, in connection with some of his evil advisers, to make his escape from his father's control entirely by secretly absconding from the country, and seeking a retreat under the protection of some foreign power. The manner in which he executed this scheme, and the consequences which finally resulted from it, will be related in the next chapter.

CHAPTER XVI

THE FLIGHT OF ALEXIS

1717

Alexis resolves to escape—Alexis makes arrangements for flight—Secrecy—Alexis deceives Afrosinia—How Alexis obtained the money—Alexander Kikin—Alexis sets out on his journey—Meets Kikin—Arrangements—Plans matured—Kikin's cunning contrivances—False letters—Kikin and Alexis concert their plans—Possibility of being intercepted—More prevarications—Arrival at Vienna—The Czar sends for Alexis—Interview with the envoys—Threats of Alexis—He returns to Naples—St. Elmo—Long negotiations—Alexis resolves at last to return—His letter to his father—Alexis delivers himself up

When Alexis received the letter from his father at Copenhagen, ordering him to proceed at once to that city and join his father there, or else to come to a definite and final conclusion in respect to the convent that he would join, he at once determined, as intimated in the last chapter, that he would avail himself of the opportunity to escape from his father's control altogether. Under pretense of obeying his father's orders that he should go to Copenhagen, he could make all the necessary preparations for leaving the country without suspicion, and then, when once across the frontier, he could go where he pleased. He determined to make his escape to a foreign court, with a view of putting himself under the protection there of some prince or potentate who, from feelings of rivalry toward his father, or from some other motive, might be disposed, he thought, to espouse his cause.

He immediately began to make arrangements for his flight. What the exact truth is in respect to the arrangements which he made could never be fully ascertained, for the chief source of information in respect to them is from confessions which Alexis made himself after he was brought back. But in these confessions he made such confusion, first confessing a little, then a little more, then contradicting himself, then admitting, when the thing had been proved against him, what he had before denied, that it was almost impossible to disentangle the truth from his confused and contradictory declarations. The substance of the case was, however, as follows:

In the first place, he determined carefully to conceal his design from all except the two or three intimate friends and advisers who originally counseled him to adopt it. He intended to take with him his concubine Afrosinia, and also a number of domestic servants and other attendants, but he did not allow any of them to know where he was going. He gave them to understand that he was going to Copenhagen to join his father. He was afraid that, if any of those persons were to know his real design, it would, in some way or other, be divulged.

As to Afrosinia, he was well aware that she would know that he could not intend to take her to Copenhagen into his father's presence, and so he deceived her as to his real design, and induced her to set out with him, without suspicion, by telling her that he was only going to take her with him a part of the way. She was only to go, he said, as far as Riga, a town on the shores of the Baltic, on the way toward Copenhagen. Alexis was the less inclined to make a confidante of Afrosinia from the fact that she had never been willingly his companion. She was a Finland girl, a captive taken in war, and preserved to be sold as a slave on account of her beauty. When she came into the possession of Alexis he forced her to submit to his will. She was a slave, and it was useless for her to resist or complain. It is said that Alexis only induced her to yield to him by drawing his knife and threatening to kill her on the spot if she made any difficulty. Thus, although he seems to have become, in the end, strongly attached to her, he never felt that she was really and cordially on his side. He accordingly, in this case, concealed from her his real designs, and told her he was only going to take her with him a little way. He would then send her back, he said, to Petersburg. So Afrosinia made arrangements to accompany him without feeling any concern.

Alexis obtained all the money that he required by borrowing considerable sums of the different members of the government and friends of his father, under pretense that he was going to his father at Copenhagen. He showed them the letter which his father had written him, and this, they thought, was sufficient authority for them to furnish him with the money. He borrowed in this way various sums of different persons, and thus obtained an abundant supply. The largest sum which he obtained from any one person was two thousand ducats, which were lent him by Prince Menzikoff, a noble who stood very high in Peter's confidence, and who had been left by him chief in command during his absence. The prince gave Alexis some advice, too, about the arrangements which he was to make for his journey, supposing all the time that he was really going to Copenhagen.

The chief instigator and adviser of Alexis in this affair was a man named Alexander Kikin. This Kikin was an officer of high rank in the navy department, under the government, and the Czar had placed great confidence in him. But he was inclined to espouse the cause of the old Muscovite party, and to hope for a revolution that would bring that party again into power. He was not at this time in St. Petersburg, but had gone forward to provide a place of retreat for Alexis. Alexis was to meet him at the town of Libau, which stands on the shores of the Baltic Sea, between St. Petersburg and Konigsberg, on the route which Alexis would have to take in going to Copenhagen. Alexis communicated with Kikin in writing, and Kikin arranged and directed all the details of the plan. He kept purposely at a distance from Alexis, to avoid suspicion.

At length, when all was ready, Alexis set out from St. Petersburg, taking with him Afrosinia and several other attendants, and journeyed to Libau. There he met Kikin, and each congratulated the other warmly on the success which had thus far attended their operations.

Alexis asked Kikin what place he had provided for him, and Kikin replied that he had made arrangements for him to go to Vienna. He had been to Vienna himself, he said, under pretense of public business committed to his charge by the Czar, and had seen and conferred with the Emperor of Germany there, and the emperor agreed to receive and protect him, and not to deliver him up to his father until some permanent and satisfactory arrangement should have been made.

"So you must go on," continued Kikin, "to Konigsberg and Dantzic; and then, instead of going forward toward Copenhagen, you will turn off on the road to Vienna, and when you get there the emperor will provide a safe place of retreat for you. When you arrive there, if your father should

Jacob Abbott

find out where you are, and send some one to try to persuade you to return home, you must not, on any account, listen to him; for, as certain as your father gets you again in his power, after your leaving the country in this way, he will have you beheaded."

Kikin contrived a number of very cunning devices for averting suspicion from himself and those really concerned in the plot, and throwing it upon innocent persons. Among other things, he induced Alexis to write several letters to different individuals in St. Petersburg—Prince Menzikoff among the rest—thanking them for the advice and assistance that they had rendered him in setting out upon his journey, which advice and assistance was given honestly, on the supposition that he was really going to his father at Copenhagen. The letters of thanks, however, which Kikin dictated were written in an ambiguous and mysterious manner, being adroitly contrived to awaken suspicion in Peter's mind, if he were to see them, that these persons were in the secret of Alexis's plans, and really intended to assist him in his escape. When the letters were written Alexis delivered them to Kikin, who at some future time, in case of necessity, was to show them to Peter, and pretend that he had intercepted them. Thus he expected to avert suspicion from himself, and throw it upon innocent persons.

Kikin also helped Alexis about writing a letter to his father from Libau, saying to him that he left St. Petersburg, and had come so far on his way toward Copenhagen. This letter was, however, not dated at Libau, where Alexis then was, but at Konigsberg, which was some distance farther on, and it was sent forward to be transmitted from that place.

When Alexis had thus arranged every thing with Kikin, he prepared to set out on his journey again. He was to go on first to Konigsberg, then to Dantzic, and there, instead of embarking on board a ship to go to Copenhagen, according to his father's plan, he was to turn off toward Vienna. It was at that point, accordingly, that his actual rebellion against his father's commands would begin. He had some misgivings about being able to reach that point. He asked Kikin what he should do in case his father should have sent somebody to meet him at Konigsberg or Dantzic.

"Why, you must join them in the first instance," said Kikin, "and pretend to be much pleased to meet them; and then you must contrive to make your escape from them in the night, either entirely alone, or only with one servant. You must abandon your baggage and every thing else.

"Or, if you can not manage to do this," continued Kikin, "you must pretend to be sick; and if there are two persons sent to meet you, you can send one of them on before, with your baggage and attendants, promising yourself to come on quietly afterward with the other; and then you can contrive to bribe the other, or in some other way induce him to escape with you, and so go to Vienna."

Alexis did not have occasion to resort to either of these expedients, for nobody was sent to meet him. He journeyed on without any interruption till he came to Konigsberg, which was the place where the road turned off to Vienna. It was now necessary to say something to Afrosinia and his other attendants to account for the new direction which his journey was to take; so he told them that he had received a letter from his father, ordering him, before proceeding to Copenhagen, to go to Vienna on some public business which was to be done there. Accordingly, when he turned off, they accompanied him without any apparent suspicion.

Alexis proceeded in this way to Vienna, and there he appealed to the emperor for protection. The emperor received him, listened to the complaints which he made against the Czar—for Alexis, as might have been expected, cast all the blame of the quarrel upon his father—and, after entertaining him for a while in different places, he provided him at last with a secret retreat in a fortress in the Tyrol.

Here Alexis concealed himself, and it was a long time before his father could ascertain what had become of him. At length the Czar learned that he was in the emperor's dominions, and he wrote with his own hand a very urgent letter to the emperor, representing the misconduct of Alexis in its true light, and demanding that he should not harbor such an undutiful and rebellious son, but should send him home. He sent two envoys to act as the bearers of this letter, and to bring Alexis back to his father in case the emperor should conclude to surrender him.

The emperor communicated the contents of this letter to Alexis, but Alexis begged him not to comply with his father's demand. He said that the difficulty was owing altogether to his father's harshness and cruelty, and that, if he were to be sent back, he should be in danger of his life from his father's violence.

After long negotiations and delays, the emperor allowed the envoys to go and visit Alexis in the place of his retreat, with a view of seeing whether they could not prevail upon him to return home with them. The envoys carried a letter to Alexis which his father had written with his own hand, representing to him, in strong terms, the impropriety and wickedness of his conduct, and the enormity of the crime which he had committed against his father by his open rebellion against his authority, and denouncing against him, if he persisted in his wicked course, the judgment of God, who had threatened in his Word to punish disobedient children with eternal death.

But all these appeals had no effect upon the stubborn will of Alexis. He declared to the envoys that he would not return with them, and he said, moreover, that the emperor had promised to protect him, and that, if his father continued to persecute him in this way, he would resist by force, and, with the aid which the emperor would render him, he would make war upon his father, depose him from his power, and raise himself to the throne in his stead.

After this there followed a long period of negotiation and delay, during which many events occurred which it would be interesting to relate if time and space permitted. Alexis was transferred from one place to another, with a view of eluding any attempt which his father might make to get possession of him again, either by violence or stratagem, and at length was conveyed to Naples, in Italy, and was concealed in the castle of St. Elmo there.

In the mean time Peter grew more and more urgent in his demands upon the emperor to deliver up his son, and the emperor at last, finding that the quarrel was really becoming serious, and being convinced, moreover, by the represen-tations which Peter caused to be made to him, that Alexis had been much more to blame than he had supposed, seemed disposed to change his ground, and began now to advise Alexis to return home. Alexis was quite alarmed when he found that, after all, he was not to be supported in his rebellion by the emperor, and at length, after a great many negotiations, difficulties, and delays, he determined to make a virtue of necessity and to go home. His father had written him repeated letters, promising him a free pardon if he would return, and threatening him in the most severe and decided manner if he did not. To the last of these letters, when Alexis had finally resolved to go back, he wrote the following very meek and submissive reply. It was written from Naples in October, 1717:

"MY CLEMENT LORD AND FATHER,—

"I have received your majesty's most gracious letter by Messrs. Tolstoi and Rumanrow,[1] in which, as also by word of mouth, I am most graciously assured of pardon for having fled without your permission in case I return. I give you most hearty thanks with tears in my eyes, and own myself unworthy of all favor. I throw myself at your feet, and implore your clemency, and beseech you to pardon my crimes, for which I acknowledge that I deserve the severest punishment. But I rely on your gracious assurances, and, submitting to your pleasure, shall set out immediately from Naples to attend your majesty at Petersburg with those whom your majesty has sent.

"Your most humble and unworthy servant, who deserves not to be called your son,

"ALEXIS."

After having written and dispatched this letter Alexis surrendered himself to Tolstoi and Rumanrow, and in their charge set out on his return to Russia, there to be delivered into his father's hands; for Peter was now in Russia, having returned there as soon as he heard of Alexis's flight.

[1] These were the envoys, officers of high rank in the government, whom Peter had sent to bring Alexis back.

CHAPTER XVII

THE TRIAL

1717-1718

His father's manifesto on his return—Interview between Alexis and his father—Anger of the Czar—Substantial cause for Peter's excitement—Grand councils convened—Scene in the hall—Conditional promise of pardon—Alexis humbled—Secret conference—Alexis disinherited—The new heir—Oaths administered—Alexis imprisoned—Investigation commenced—Prisoners—The torture—Arrest of Kikin—The page—He fails to warn Kikin in time—Condemnation of prisoners—Executions—Dishonest confessions of Alexis—His excesses—Result of the examinations—Proofs against Alexis—An admission—Testimony of Afrosinia

As soon as Alexis arrived in the country, his father issued a manifesto, in which he gave a long and full account of his son's misdemeanors and crimes, and of the patient and persevering, but fruitless efforts which he himself had made to reclaim him, and announced his determination to cut him off from the succession to the crown as wholly and hopelessly irreclaimable. This manifesto was one of the most remarkable documents that history records. It concluded with deposing Alexis from all his rights as son and heir to his

Jacob Abbott

father, and appointing his younger brother Peter, the little son of Catharine, as inheritor in his stead; and finally laying the paternal curse upon Alexis if he ever thereafter pretended to, or in any way claimed the succession of which he had been deprived.

This manifesto was issued as soon as Peter learned that Alexis had arrived in the country under the charge of the officers who had been appointed to bring him, and before the Czar had seen him. Alexis continued his journey to Moscow, where the Czar then was. When he arrived he went that same night to the palace, and there had a long conference with his father. He was greatly alarmed and overawed by the anger which his father expressed, and he endeavored very earnestly, by expressions of penitence and promises of amendment, to appease him. But it was now too late. The ire of the Czar was thoroughly aroused, and he could not be appeased. He declared that he was fully resolved on deposing his son, as he had announced in his manifesto, and that the necessary steps for making the act of deposition in a formal and solemn manner, so as to give it full legal validity as a measure of state, would be taken on the following day.

It must be confessed that the agitation and anger which Peter now manifested were not wholly without excuse, for the course which Alexis had pursued had been the means of exposing his father to a great and terrible danger—to that, namely, of a rebellion among his subjects. Peter did not even know but that such a rebellion was already planned and was ripe for execution, and that it might not break out at any time, notwithstanding his having succeeded in recovering possession of the person of Alexis, and in bringing him home. Of such a rebellion, if one had been planned, the name of Alexis would have been, of course, the watch-word and rallying-point, and Peter had a great deal of ground for apprehension that such a one had been extensively organized and was ready to be carried into effect. He immediately set himself at work to ferret out the whole affair, resolving, however, in the first place, to disable Alexis himself from doing any farther mischief by destroying finally and forever all claims on his part to the inheritance of the crown.

Accordingly, on the following morning, before daybreak, the garrison of the city were put under arms, and a regiment of the Guards was posted around the palace, so as to secure all the gates and avenues; and orders were sent, at the same time, to the principal ministers, nobles, and counselors of state, to repair to the great hall in the castle, and to the bishops and clergy to assemble in the Cathedral. Every body knew that the occasion on which they were convened was that they might witness the disinheriting of the prince imperial by his father, in consequence of his vices and crimes; and in coming together in obedience to the summons, the minds of all men were filled with solemn awe, like those of men assembling to witness an execution.

When the appointed hour arrived the great bell was tolled, and Alexis was brought into the hall of the castle, where the nobles were assembled, bound as a prisoner, and deprived of his sword. The Czar himself stood at the upper end of the hall, surrounded by the chief officers of state. Alexis was brought before him. As he approached he presented a writing to his father, and then fell down on his knees before him, apparently overwhelmed with grief and shame.

The Czar handed the paper to one of his officers who stood near, and then asked Alexis what it was that he desired. Alexis, in reply, begged that his father would have mercy upon him and spare his life. The Czar said that he would spare his life, and forgive him for all his treasonable and rebellious acts, on condition that he would make a full and complete confession, without any restriction or reserve, of every thing connected with his late escape from the country, explaining fully all the details of the plan which he had formed, and reveal the names of all his advisers and accomplices. But if his confession was not full and complete—if he suppressed or concealed any thing, or the name of any person concerned in the affair or privy to it, then this promise of pardon should be null and void.

The Czar also said that Alexis must renounce the succession to the crown, and must confirm the renunciation by a solemn oath, and acknowledge it by signing a declaration, in writing, to that effect with his own hand. To all this, Alexis, who seemed overwhelmed with contrition and anguish, solemnly agreed, and declared that he was ready to make a full and complete confession.

The Czar then asked his son who it was that advised him and aided him in his late escape from the kingdom. Alexis seemed unwilling to reply to this question in the midst of such an assemblage, but said something to his father in a low voice, which the others could not hear. In consequence of what he thus said his father took him into an adjoining room, and there conversed with him in private for a few minutes, and then both returned together into the public hall. It is supposed that while they were thus apart Alexis gave his father the names of some of those who had aided and abetted him in his absconding, for immediately afterward three couriers were dispatched in three different directions, as if with orders to arrest the persons who were thus accused.

As soon as Alexis and his father had returned into the hall, the document was produced which the prince was to sign, renouncing the succession to the crown. The signature and seal of Alexis were affixed to this document with all due formality. Then a declaration was made on the part of the Czar, stating the reasons which had induced his majesty to depose his eldest son from the succession, and to appoint his younger son, Peter, in his place. This being done, all the officers present were required to make a solemn oath on the Gospels, and to sign a written declaration, of which several copies had previously been prepared, importing that the Czar, having excluded from the crown his son Alexis, and appointed his son Peter his successor in his stead, they owned the legality and binding force of the decree, acknowledged Peter as the true and rightful heir, and bound themselves to stand by him with their lives against any or all who should oppose him, and declared that they never would, under any pretense whatsoever, adhere to Alexis, or assist him in recovering the succession.

The whole company then repaired to the Cathedral, where the bishops and other ecclesiastics were assembled, and there the whole body of the clergy solemnly took the same oath and subscribed the same declaration. The same oath was also afterward administered to all the officers of the army, governors of the provinces, and other public functionaries throughout the empire.

When these ceremonies at the palace and at the Cathedral were concluded, the company dispersed. Alexis was placed in confinement in one of the palaces in Moscow, and none were allowed to have access to him except those whom the Czar appointed to keep him in charge.

Immediately after this the necessary proceedings for a full investigation of the whole affair were commenced in a formal and solemn manner. A series of questions were drawn up and given to Alexis, that he might make out deliberate answers to them in writing. Grand courts of investigation and inquiry were convened in Moscow, the great dignitaries both of Church and state being summoned from all parts of the empire to attend them. These persons came to the capital in great state, and, in going to and fro to attend at the halls of judgment from day to day, they moved through the streets with such a degree of pomp and parade as to attract great crowds of spectators. As fast as the names were discovered of persons who were implicated in Alexis's escape, or who were suspected of complicity in it, officers were dispatched to arrest them. Some were taken from their beds at midnight, without a moment's warning, and shut up in dungeons in a great fortress at Moscow. When questioned, if they seemed inclined to return evasive answers, or to withhold any information of which the judges thought they were possessed, they were taken into the torturing-room and put to the torture.

One of the first who was arrested was Alexander Kikin, who had been Alexis's chief confidant and adviser in all his proceedings. Kikin had taken extreme precautions to guard against having his agency in the affair found out; but Alexis, in the answers that he gave to the first series of questions that were put to him, betrayed him. Kikin was aware of the danger, and, in order to secure for himself some chance of escape in case Alexis should make disclosures implicating him, had bribed a page, who was always in close attendance upon the Czar, to let him know immediately in case of any movement to arrest him.

The name of this page was Baklanoffsky. He was in the apartment at the time that the Czar was writing the order for Kikin's arrest, standing, as was his wont, behind the chair of the Czar, so as to be ready at hand to convey messages or to wait upon his master. He looked over, and saw the order which the Czar was writing. He immediately contrived some excuse to leave the apartment, and hurrying away, he went to the post-house and sent on an express by post to Kikin at Petersburg to warn him of the danger.

But the Czar, noticing his absence, sent some one off after him, and thus his errand at the post-house was discovered, but not until after the express had gone. Another express was immediately sent off with the order for Kikin's arrest, and both the couriers arrived in Petersburg very nearly at the same time. The one, however, who brought the warning was a little too late. When he arrived the house of the commissioner was surrounded by a guard of fifty grenadiers, and officers were then in Kikin's apartment taking him out of his bed. They put him at once in irons and took him away, scarcely allowing him time to bid his wife farewell.

The page was, of course, arrested and sent to prison too. A number of other persons, many of whom were of very high rank, were arrested in a similar manner.

The arrival of Alexis at Moscow took place early in February, and nearly all of February and March were occupied with these arrests and the proceedings of the court in trying the prisoners. At length, toward the end of March, a considerable number, Kikin himself being among them, were condemned to death, and executed in the most dreadful manner in a great public square in the centre of Moscow. One was impaled alive; that is, a great stake was driven through his body into the ground, and he was left in that situation to die. Others were broken on the wheel. One, a bishop, was burnt. The heads of the principal offenders were afterward cut off and set up on poles at the four corners of a square inclosure made for the purpose, the impaled body lying in the middle.

The page who had been bribed by Kikin was not put to death. His life was spared, perhaps on account of his youth, but he was very severely punished by scourging.

During all this time Alexis continued to be confined to his

prison, and he was subjected to repeated examinations and cross-examinations, in order to draw from him not only the whole truth in respect to his own motives and designs in his flight, but also such information as might lead to the full development of the plans and designs of the party in Russia who were opposed to the government of Peter, and who had designed to make use of the name and position of Alexis for the accomplishment of their schemes. Alexis had promised to make a full and complete confession, but he did not do so. In the answers to the series of questions which were first addressed to him, he confessed as much as he thought was already known, and endeavored to conceal the rest. In a short time, however, many things that he had at first denied or evaded were fully proved by other testimony taken in the trial of the prisoners who have already been referred to. Then Alexis was charged with the omissions or evasions in his confession which had thus been made to appear, and asked for an explanation, and thereupon he made new confessions, acknowledging the newly-discovered facts, and excusing himself for not having mentioned them before by saying that he had forgotten them, or else that he was afraid to divulge them for fear of injuring the persons that would be implicated by them. Thus he went on contradicting and involving himself more and more by every fresh confession, until, at last, his father, and all the judges who had convened to investigate the case, ceased to place any confidence in any thing that he said, and lost almost all sympathy for him in his distress.

The examination was protracted through many months. The result of it, on the whole, was, that it was fully proved that there was a powerful party in Russia opposed to the reforms and improvements of the Czar, and particularly to the introduction of the European civilization into the country, who were desirous of effecting a revolution, and who wished to avail themselves of the quarrel between Alexis and his father to promote their schemes. Alexis was too much stupefied by his continual drunkenness to take any very active or intelligent part in these schemes, but he was more or less distinctly aware of them; and in the offers which he had made to enter a monastery and renounce all claims to the crown he had been utterly insincere, his only object having been to blind his father by means of them and gain time. He acknowledged that he had hated his father, and had wished for his death, and when he fled to Vienna it was his intention to remain until he could return and take possession of the empire in his father's place. He, however, solemnly declared that it was never his intention to take any steps himself toward that end during his father's lifetime, though he admitted, at last, when the fact had been pretty well proved against him by other evidence, that, in case an insurrection in his behalf had broken out in Russia, and he had been called upon, he should have joined the rebels.

A great deal of information, throwing light upon the plans of Alexis and of the conspirators in Russia connected with him, was obtained from the disclosures made by Afrosinia. As has already been stated, she had been taken by Alexis as a slave, and forced, against her will, to join herself to him and to follow his fortunes. He had never admitted her into his confidence, but had induced her, from time to time, to act as he desired by telling her any falsehood which would serve the purpose. She consequently was not bound to him by any ties of honor or affection, and felt herself at liberty to answer freely all questions which were put to her by the judges. Her testimony was of great value in many points, and contributed very essentially toward elucidating the whole affair.

Jacob Abbott

CHAPTER XVIII

THE CONDEMNATION AND DEATH OF ALEXIS

1718

Condition of Alexis—The two tribunals—Their powers—The Czar calls for a decision—His addresses to the two councils—Deliberation of the clergy—Their answer—Their quotations from Scripture—Cautious language used by the bishops—They suggest clemency and mercy—Additional confessions made by Alexis—The priest—Tolstoi sent to Alexis—The Czar's three final questions—Alexis's three answers—His account of the manner in which he had been educated—His feelings toward his father—His attempts to maim himself—His treasonable designs—Alexis's confession sent to the council—Decision of the council—The promise of pardon—Forfeiture of it—Conclusion of the sentence—The signatures—The 6th of July—The Czar's mental struggles—Alexis brought out to hear his sentence—Overwhelmed with dismay—Visit of his father—Sorrowful scene—Alexis sends a second time for his father—His death—Czar's circular—The body laid in state—Rumors circulated—Funeral cere-monies—The opposition broken up—The mother of Alexis—Afrosinia—The Czar pardons her

The examinations and investigations described in the last

chapter were protracted through a period of several months. They were commenced in February, and were not concluded until June. During all this time Alexis had been kept in close confinement, except when he had been brought out before his judges for the various examinations and cross-examinations to which he had been subjected; and as the truth in respect to his designs became more and more fully developed, and the danger in respect to the result increased, he sank gradually into a state of distress and terror almost impossible to be conceived.

The tribunals before whom he was tried were not the regular judicial tribunals of the country. They were, on the other hand, two grand convocations of all the great official dignitaries of the Church and of the state, that were summoned expressly for this purpose—not to *decide* the case, for, according to the ancient customs of the Russian empire, that was the sole and exclusive province of the Czar, but to aid him in investigating it, and then, if called upon, to give him their counsel in respect to the decision of it. One of these assemblies consisted of the ecclesiastical authorities, the archbishops, the bishops, and other dignitaries of the Church. The other was composed of nobles, ministers of state, officers of the army and navy in high command, and other great civil and military functionaries. These two assemblies met and deliberated in separate halls, and pursued their investigations in respect to the several persons implicated in the affair, as they were successively brought before them, under the direction of the Czar, though the final disposal of each case rested, it was well understood, with him alone.

At length, in the month of June, when all the other cases had been disposed of, and the proof in respect to Alexis was considered complete, the Czar sent in a formal address to each of these conventions, asking their opinion and advice in respect to what he ought to do with his son.

In his address to the archbishops and bishops, he stated that, although he was well aware that he had himself absolute power to judge his son for his crimes, and to dispose of him according to his own will and pleasure, without asking advice of any one, still, "as men were sometimes less discerning," he said, "in their own affairs than in those of others, so that even the most skillful physicians do not run the hazard of prescribing for themselves, but call in the assistance of others when they are indisposed," in the same manner he, having the fear of God before his eyes, and being afraid to offend him, had decided to bring the question at issue between himself and his son before them, that they might examine the Word of God in relation to it, and give their opinion, in writing, what the will of God in such a case might be. He wished also, he said, that the opinion to which they should come should be signed by each one of them individually, with his own hand.

He made a similar statement in his address to the grand council of civil authorities, calling upon them also to give their opinion in respect to what should be done with Alexis. "I beg of you," he said, in the conclusion of his address, "to consider of the affair, to examine it seriously and with attention, and see what it is that our son has deserved, without flattering me, or apprehending that, if in your judgment he deserves no more than slight punishment, it will be disagreeable to me; for I swear to you, by the Great God and by his judgments, that you have nothing to fear from me on this account.

"Neither are you to allow the consideration that it is the son of your sovereign that you are to pass judgment upon to have any effect upon you. But do justice without respect of persons, so that your conscience and mine may not reproach us at the great day of judgment."

The convocation of clergy, in deliberating upon the answer which they were to make to the Czar, deemed it advisable to proceed with great caution. They were not quite willing to recommend directly and openly that Alexis should be put to death, while, at the same time, they wished to give the sanction of their approval for any measures of severity which the Czar might be inclined to take. So they forbore to express any positive opinion of their own, but contented themselves with looking out in the Scriptures, both in the Old and New Testament, the terrible denunciations which are therein contained against disobedient and rebellious children, and the accounts of fearful punishments which were inflicted upon them in Jewish history. They began their statement by formally acknowledging that Peter himself had absolute power to dispose of the case of his son according to his own sovereign will and pleasure; that they had no jurisdiction in the case, and could not presume to pronounce judgment, or say any thing which could in any way restrain or limit the Czar in doing what he judged best. But nevertheless, as the Czar had graciously asked them for their counsel as a means of instructing his own mind previously to coming to a decision, they would proceed to quote from the Holy Scriptures such passages as might be considered to bear upon the subject, and to indicate the will of God in respect to the action of a sovereign and father in such a case.

They then proceeded to quote the texts and passages of Scripture. Some of these texts were denunciations of rebellious and disobedient children, such as, "The eye that mocketh his father and that despiseth to obey his mother, the ravens of the valley shall pluck it out," and the Jewish law providing that, "If a man have a stubborn and rebellious son, who will not obey the voice of his father nor the voice of his mother, and that, when they have chastened him, will not

Jacob Abbott

hearken unto them, then shall his father and mother lay hold of him, and bring him out unto the elders of his city, and unto the gate of his place, and shall say unto the elders of his city, This our son is rebellious: he will not obey our voice; he is a glutton and a drunkard. And all the men of his city shall stone him with stones that he die."

There were other passages quoted relating to actual cases which occurred in the Jewish history of sons being punished with death for crimes committed against their parents, such as that of Absalom, and others.

The bearing and tendency of all these extracts from the Scriptures was to justify the severest possible treatment of the unhappy criminal. The bishops added, however, at the close of their communication, that they had made these extracts in obedience to the command of their sovereign, not by way of pronouncing sentence, or making a decree, or in any other way giving any authoritative decision on the question at issue, but only to furnish to the Czar himself such spiritual guidance and instruction in the case as the word of God afforded. It would be very far from their duty, they said, to condemn any one to death, for Jesus Christ had taught his ministers not to be governed by a spirit of anger, but by a spirit of meekness. They had no power to condemn any one to death, or to seek his blood. That, when necessary, was the province of the civil power. Theirs was to bring men to repentance of their sins, and to offer them forgiveness of the same through Jesus Christ their Savior.

They therefore, in submitting their communication to his imperial majesty, did it only that he might do what seemed right in his own eyes. "If he concludes to punish his fallen son," they said, "according to his deeds, and in a manner proportionate to the enormity of his crimes, he has before him the declarations and examples which we have herein drawn from the Scriptures of the Old Testament. If, on the other hand, he is inclined to mercy, he has the example of Jesus Christ, who represented the prodigal son as received and forgiven when he returned and repented, who dismissed the woman taken in adultery, when by the law she deserved to be stoned, and who said that he would have mercy and not sacrifice."

The document concluded by the words,

"The heart of the Czar is in the hand of God, and may he choose the part to which the hand of God shall turn it."

As for the other assembly, the one composed of the nobles and senators, and other great civil and military functionaries, before rendering their judgment they caused Alexis to be brought before them again, in order to call for additional explanations, and to see if he still adhered to the confessions that he had made. At these audiences Alexis confirmed what he had before said, and acknowledged more freely than he had done before the treasonable intentions of which he had been guilty. His spirit seems by this time to have been completely broken, and he appeared to have thought that the only hope for him of escape from death was in the most humble and abject confessions and earnest supplications for pardon. In these his last confessions, too, he implicated some persons who had not before been accused. One was a certain priest named James. Alexis said that at one time he was confessing to this priest, and, among other sins which he mentioned, he said "that he wished for the death of his father." The priest's reply to this was, as Alexis said, "God will pardon you for that, my son, for we all," meaning the priests, "wish it too." The priest was immediately arrested, but, on being questioned, he denied having made any such reply. The inquisitors then put him to the torture, and there forced from him the admission that he had spoken those words. Whether he had really spoken them, or only admitted it to put an end to the torture, it is impossible to say.

They asked him for the names of the persons whom he had heard express a desire that the Czar should die, but he said he could not recollect. He had heard it from several persons, but he could not remember who they were. He said that Alexis was a great favorite among the people, and that they sometimes used to drink his health under the designation of the Hope of Russia.

The Czar himself also obtained a final and general acknowledgment of guilt from his son, which he sent in to the senate on the day before their judgment was to be rendered. He obtained this confession by sending Tolstoi, an officer of the highest rank in his court, and the person who had been the chief medium of the intercourse and of the communications which he had held with his son during the whole course of the affair, with the following written instructions:

"To M. TOLSTOI, PRIVY COUNSELOR:

"Go to my son this afternoon, and put down in writing the answers he shall give to the following questions:

"I. What is the reason why he has always been so disobedient to me, and has refused to do what I required of him, or to apply himself to any useful business, notwithstanding all the guilt and shame which he has incurred by so strange and unusual a course?

"II. Why is it that he has been so little afraid of me, and has not apprehended the consequences that must inevitably follow from his disobedience?

"III. What induced him to desire to secure possession of the crown otherwise than by obedience to me, and following me in the natural order of succession? And examine him upon every thing else that bears any relation to this affair."

Tolstoi went to Alexis in the prison, and read these questions to him. Alexis wrote out the following statement in reply to them, which Tolstoi carried to the Czar:

"I. Although I was well aware that to be disobedient as I was to my father, and refuse to do what please him, was a very strange and unusual course, and both a sin and a shame, yet I was led into it, in the first instance, in consequence of having been brought up from my infancy with a governess and her maids, from whom I learned nothing but amusements, and diversions, and bigotry, to which I had naturally an inclination.

"The person to whom I was intrusted after I was removed from my governess gave me no better instructions.

"My father, afterward being anxious about my education, and desirous that I should apply myself to what became the son of the Czar, ordered me to learn the German language and other sciences, which I was very averse to. I applied myself to them in a very negligent manner, and only pretended to study at all in order to gain time, and without having any inclination to learn any thing.

"And as my father, who was then frequently with the army, was absent from me a great deal, he ordered his serene highness, the Prince Menzikoff, to have an eye upon me. While he was with me I was obliged to apply myself, but, as soon as I was out of his sight, the persons with whom I was left, observing that I was only bent on bigotry and idleness, on keeping company with priests and monks, and drinking with them, they not only encouraged me to neglect my business, but took pleasure in doing as I did. As these persons had been about me from my infancy, I was accustomed to observe their directions, to fear them, and to comply with their wishes in every thing, and thus, by degrees, they alienated my affections from my father by diverting me with pleasures of this nature; so that, by little and little, I came to have not only the military affairs and other actions of my father in horror, but also his person itself, which made me always wish to be at a distance from him. Alexander Kikin especially, when he was with me, took a great deal of pains to confirm me in this way of life.

"My father, having compassion on me, and desiring still to make me worthy of the state to which I was called, sent me into foreign countries; but, as I was already grown to man's estate, I made no alteration in my way of living.

"It is true, indeed, that my travels were of some advantage to me, but they were insufficient to erase the vicious habits which had taken such deep root in me.

"II. It was this evil disposition which prevented my being apprehensive of my father's correction for my disobedience. I was really afraid of him, but it was not with a filial fear. I only sought for means to get away from him, and was in no wise concerned to do his will, but to avoid, by every means in my power, what he required of me. Of this I will now freely confess one plain instance.

"When I came back to Petersburg to my father from abroad, at the end of one of my journeys, he questioned me about my studies, and, among other things, asked me if I had forgotten what I had learned, and I told him no. He then asked me to bring him some of my drawings of plans. Then, fearing that he would order me to draw something in his presence, which

I could not do, as I knew nothing of the matter, I set to work to devise a way to hurt my hand so that it should be impossible for me to do any thing at all. So I charged a pistol with ball, and, taking it in my left hand, I let it off against the palm of my right, with a design to have shot through it. The ball, however, missed my hand, though the powder burned it sufficiently to wound it. The ball entered the wall of my room, and it may be seen there still.

"My father, observing my hand to be wounded, asked me how it came. I told him an evasive story, and kept the truth to myself. By this means you may see that I was afraid of my father, but not with a proper filial fear.[1]

"III. As to my having desired to obtain the crown otherwise than by obedience to my father, and following him in regular order of succession, all the world may easily understand the reason; for, when I was once out of the right way, and resolved to imitate my father in nothing, I naturally sought to obtain the succession by any, even the most wrongful method. I confess that I was even willing to come into possession of it by foreign assistance, if it had been necessary. If the emperor had been ready to fulfill the promise that he made me of procuring for me the crown of Russia, even with an armed force, I should have spared nothing to have obtained it.

"For instance, if the emperor had demanded that I should afterward furnish him with Russian troops against any of his enemies, in exchange for his service in aiding me, or large sums of money, I should have done whatever he pleased. I would have given great presents to his ministers and generals over and above. In a word, I would have thought nothing too much to have obtained my desire."

This confession, after it was brought to the Czar by Tolstoi,

Jacob Abbott

to whom Alexis gave it, was sent by him to the great council of state, to aid them in forming their opinion.

The council were occupied for the space of a week in hearing the case, and then they drew up and signed their decision.

The statement which they made began by acknowledging that they had not of themselves any original right to try such a question, the Czar himself, according to the ancient constitution of the empire, having sole and exclusive jurisdiction in all such affairs, without being beholden to his subjects in regard to them in any manner whatever; but, nevertheless, as the Czar had deemed it expedient to refer it to them, they accepted the responsibility, and, after having fully investigated the case, were now ready to pronounce judgment.

They then proceeded to declare that, after a full hearing and careful consideration of all the evidence, both oral and written, which had been laid before them, including the confessions of Alexis himself, they found that he had been guilty of treason and rebellion against his father and sovereign, and deserved to suffer death.

"And although," said the council, in continuation, "although, both before and since his return to Russia, the Czar his father had promised him pardon on certain conditions, yet those conditions were particularly and expressly specified, especially the one which provided that he should make a full and complete confession of all his designs, and of the names of all the persons who had been privy to them or concerned in the execution of them. With these conditions, and particularly the last, Alexis had not complied, but had returned insincere and evasive answers to the questions which had been put to him, and had concealed not only the names of a great many of the principal persons that were involved in the conspiracy, but also the most important designs and intentions of the conspirators, thus making it appear that he had determined to reserve to himself an opportunity hereafter, when a favorable occasion should present itself, of resuming his designs and putting his wicked enterprise into execution against his sovereign and father. He thus had rendered himself unworthy of the pardon which his father had promised him, and had forfeited all claim to it."

The sentence of the council concluded in the following words:

"It is with hearts full of affliction and eyes streaming down with tears that we, as subjects and servants, pronounce this sentence, considering that, being such, it does not belong to us to enter into a judgment of so great importance, and particularly to pronounce sentence against the son of the most mighty and merciful Czar our lord. However, since it has been his will that we should enter into judgment, we herein declare our real opinion, and pronounce this condemnation, with a conscience so pure and Christian that we think we can answer for it at the terrible, just, and impartial judgment of the Great God.

"To conclude, we submit this sentence which we now give, and the condemnation which we make, to the sovereign power and will, and to the merciful review of his Czarian majesty, our most merciful monarch."

This document was signed in the most solemn manner by all the members of the council, nearly one hundred in number. Among the signatures are the names of a great number of ministers of state, counselors, senators, governors, generals, and other personages of high civil and military rank. The document, when thus formally authenticated, was sent, with much solemn and imposing ceremony, to the Czar.

The Czar, after an interval of great suspense and solicitude, during which he seems to have endured much mental suffering, confirmed the judgment of the council, and a day was appointed on which Alexis was to be arraigned, in order that sentence of death, in accordance with it, might be solemnly pronounced upon him.

The day appointed was the 6th of July, nearly a fortnight after the judgment of the court was rendered to the Czar. The length of this delay indicates a severe struggle in the mind of the Czar between his pride and honor as a sovereign, feelings which prompted him to act in the most determined and rigorous manner in punishing a rebel against his government, and what still remained of his parental affection for his son. He knew well that after what had passed there could never be any true and genuine reconciliation, and that, as long as his son lived, his name would be the watchword of opposition and rebellion, and his very existence would act as a potent and perpetual stimulus to the treasonable designs which the foes of civilization and progress were always disposed to form. He finally, therefore, determined that the sentence of death should at least be pronounced. What his intention was in respect to the actual execution of it can never be known.

When the appointed day arrived a grand session of the council was convened, and Alexis was brought out from the fortress where he was imprisoned, and arraigned before it for the last time. He was attended by a strong guard. On being placed at the bar of the tribunal, he was called upon to repeat the confessions which he had made, and then the sentence of death, as it had been sent to the Czar, was read to him. He was then taken back again to his prison as before.

Alexis was overwhelmed with terror and distress at finding himself thus condemned; and the next morning intelligence was brought to the Czar that, after suffering convulsions at intervals through the night, he had fallen into an apoplectic fit. About noon another message was brought, saying that he had revived in some measure from the fit, yet his vital powers seemed to be sinking away, and the physician thought that his life was in great danger.

The Czar sent for the principal ministers of state to come to him, and he waited with them in great anxiety and agitation for farther tidings.

At length a third messenger came, and said that it was thought that Alexis could not possibly outlive the evening, and that he longed to see his father. The Czar immediately requested the ministers to accompany him, and set out from his palace to go to the fortress where Alexis was confined. On entering the room where his dying son was lying, he was greatly moved, and Alexis himself, bursting into tears, folded his hands and began to entreat his father's forgiveness for his sins against him. He said that he had grievously and heinously offended the majesty of God Almighty and of the Czar; that he hoped he should not recover from his illness, for if he should recover he should feel that he was unworthy to live. But he begged and implored his father, for God's sake, to take off the curse that he had pronounced against him, to forgive him for all the heinous crimes which he had committed, to bestow upon him his paternal blessing, and to cause prayers to be put up for his soul.

While Alexis was speaking thus, the Czar himself, and all the ministers and officers who had come with him, were melted in tears. The Czar replied kindly to him. He referred, it is true, to the sins and crimes of which Alexis had been guilty, but he gave him his forgiveness and his blessing, and then took his leave with tears and lamentations which rendered it impossible for him to speak, and in which all present joined. The scene was heart-rending.

Jacob Abbott

At five o'clock in the evening a major of the Guards came across the water from the fortress to the Czar's palace with a message that Alexis was extremely desirous to see his father once more. The Czar was at first unwilling to comply with this request. He could not bear, he thought, to renew the pain of such an interview. But his ministers advised him to go. They represented to him that it was hard to deny such a request from his dying son, who was probably tormented by the stings of a guilty conscience, and felt relieved and comforted when his father was near. So Peter consented to go. But just as he was going on board the boat which was to take him over to the fortress, another messenger came saying that it was too late. Alexis had expired.

On the next day after the death of his son, the Czar, in order to anticipate and preclude the false rumors in respect to the case which he knew that his enemies would endeavor to spread throughout the Continent, caused a brief but full statement of his trial and condemnation, and of the circumstances of his death, to be drawn up and sent to all his ministers abroad, in order that they might communicate the facts in an authentic form to the courts to which they were respectfully accredited.[2]

The ninth day of July, the third day after the death of Alexis, was appointed for the funeral. The body was laid in a coffin covered with black velvet. A pall of rich gold tissue was spread over the coffin, and in this way the body was conveyed to the church of the Holy Trinity, where it was laid in state. It remained in this condition during the remainder of that day and all of the next, and also on the third day until evening. It was visited by vast crowds of people, who were permitted to come up and kiss the hands of the deceased.

On the evening of the third day after the body was conveyed to the church, the funeral service was performed, and the body was conveyed to the tomb. A large procession, headed by the Czar, the Czarina, and all the chief nobility of the court, followed in the funeral train. The Czar and all the other mourners carried in their hands a small wax taper burning. The ladies were all dressed in black silks. It was said by those who were near enough in the procession to observe the Czar that he went weeping all the way.

At the service in the church a funeral sermon was pronounced by the priest from the very appropriate text, "O Absalom! my son! my son Absalom!"

Thus ended this dreadful tragedy. The party who had been opposed to the reforms and improvements of the Czar seems to have become completely disorganized after the death of Alexis, and they never again attempted to organize any resistance to Peter's plans. Indeed, most of the principal leaders had been executed or banished to Siberia. As to Ottokesa, the first wife of the Czar, and the mother of Alexis, who was proved to have been privy to his designs, she was sent away to a strong castle, and shut up for the rest of her days in a dungeon. So close was her confinement that even her food was put in to her through a hole in the wall.

It remains only to say one word in conclusion in respect to Afrosinia. When Alexis was first arrested, it was supposed that she, having been the slave and companion of Alexis, was a party with him in his treasonable designs; but in the course of the examinations it appeared very fully that whatever of connection with the affair, or participation in it, she may have had, was involuntary and innocent, and the testimony which she gave was of great service in unraveling the mystery of the whole transaction. In the end, the Czar expressed his satisfaction with her conduct in strong terms. He gave her a full pardon for the involuntary aid which she had rendered Alexis in carrying out his plans. He ordered every thing which had been taken away from her to be restored, made her presents of handsome jewelry, and said that if she would like to be married he would give her a handsome portion out of the royal treasury. But she promptly declined this proposal. "I have been compelled," she said, "to yield to one man's will by force; henceforth no other shall ever come near my side."

[1] This incident shows to what a reckless and brutal state of desperation Alexis had been reduced by the obstinacy of his opposition to his father, and by the harshness of his father's treatment of him. He confessed, on another occasion, that he had often taken medicine to produce an apparent sickness, in order to have an excuse for not attending to duties which his father required of him.

[2] There were, in fact, a great many rumors put in circulation, and they spread very far, and were continued in circulation a long time. One story was that Alexis was poisoned. Another, that his father killed him with his own hands in the prison. It was said in London that he beat him to death with an iron chain. The extent to which these and similar stories received currency indicates pretty clearly what ideas prevailed in men's minds at that time in respect to the savage ferocity of Peter's character.

CHAPTER XIX

CONCLUSION

1719-1725

Death of little Peter—Excessive grief of the Czar—The Czar shuts himself up—Device of his minister—Subsequent reign —His plan for the succession—Oath required of the people— Prince Naraskin—Proclamation—Catharine's usefulness— Splendour of the preparations—The interior of the church— The dais—The canopy—The regalia—The ceremonies— Sickness and death of Peter—Natalia—The double funeral— General character of Peter—Compared with other sovereigns—Playful vein in his character—Examples—The Little Grandfather—Taken to Cronstadt—Triumphal procession—Display before the fleet—Closing festivities— Catharine proclaimed empress—Catharine's brief reign—Her beneficent character

At the time of the death of Alexis the Czar's hopes in respect to a successor fell upon his little son, Peter Petrowitz, the child of Catharine, who was born about the time of the death of Alexis's wife, when the difficulties between himself and Alexis were first beginning to assume an alarming form. This child was now about three years old, but he was of a very weak and sickly constitution, and the Czar watched him with fear and trembling. His apprehensions proved to be well founded, for about a year after the unhappy death of Alexis he also died.

Peter was entirely overwhelmed with grief at this new calamity. He was seized with the convulsions to which he was subject when under any strong excitement, his face was distorted, and his neck was twisted and stiffened in a most frightful manner. In ordinary attacks of this kind Catharine had power to soothe and allay the spasmodic action of the muscles, and gradually release her husband from the terrible gripe of the disease, but now he would not suffer her to come near him. He could not endure it, for the sight of her renewed so vividly the anguish that he felt for the loss of their child, that it made the convulsions and the suffering worse than before.

It is said that on this occasion Peter shut himself up alone for three days and three nights in his own chamber, where he lay stretched on the ground in anguish and agony, and would not allow any body to come in. At length one of his ministers of state came, and, speaking to him through the door, appealed to him, in the most earnest manner, to come forth and give them directions in respect to the affairs of the empire, which, he said, urgently required his attention. The minister had brought with him a large number of senators to support and enforce his appeal. At length the Czar allowed the door to be opened, and the minister, with all the senators, came together into the room. The sudden appearance of so many persons, and the boldness of the minister in taking this decided step, made such an impression on the mind of the Czar as to divert his mind for the moment from his grief, and he allowed himself to be led forth and to be persuaded to take some food.

The death of Petrowitz took place in 1719, and the Czar continued to live and reign himself after this period for about sixteen [Transcriber's note: six? (Peter died in 1725)] years. During all that time he went on vigorously and successfully in completing the reforms which he had undertaken in the internal condition of his empire, and increasing the power and influence of his government among surrounding nations. He had no farther serious difficulty with the opponents of his policy, though he was always under apprehensions that difficulties might arise after his death. He had the right, according to the ancient constitution of the monarchy, to designate his own successor, choosing for this purpose either one of his sons or any other person. And now, since both his sons were dead, his mind revolved anxiously the question what provision he should make for the government of the empire after his decease. He finally concluded to leave it in the hands of Catharine herself, and, to prepare the way for this, he resolved to cause her to be solemnly crowned empress during his lifetime.

As a preliminary measure, however, before publicly announcing Catharine as his intended successor, Peter required all the officers of the empire, both civil and military, and all the nobles and other chief people of the country, to subscribe a solemn declaration and oath that they acknowledged the right of the Czar to appoint his successor, and that after his death they would sustain and defend whomsoever he should name as their emperor and sovereign.

This declaration, printed forms of which were sent all over the kingdom, was signed by the people very readily. No one, however, imagined that Catharine would be the person on whom the Czar's choice would fall. It was generally supposed that a certain Prince Naraskin would be appointed to the succession. The Czar himself said nothing of his intention, but waited until the time should arrive for carrying it into effect.

Jacob Abbott

The first step to be taken in carrying the measure into effect was to issue a grand proclamation announcing his design and explaining the reasons for it. In this proclamation Peter cited many instances from history in which great sovereigns had raised their consorts to a seat on the throne beside them, and then he recapitulated the great services which Catharine had rendered to him and to the state, which made her peculiarly deserving of such an honor. She had been a tried and devoted friend and counselor to him, he said, for many years. She had shared his labors and fatigues, had accompanied him on his journeys, and had even repeatedly encountered all the discomforts and dangers of the camp in following him in his military campaigns. By so doing she had rendered him the most essential service, and on one occasion she had been the means of saving his whole army from destruction. He therefore declared his intention of joining her with himself in the supreme power, and to celebrate this event by a solemn coronation.

The place where the coronation was to be performed was, of course, the ancient city of Moscow, and commands were issued to all the great dignitaries of Church and state, and invitations to all the foreign embassadors, to repair to that city, and be ready on the appointed day to take part in the ceremony.

It would be impossible to describe or to conceive, without witnessing it, the gorgeousness and splendor of the spectacle which the coronation afforded. The scene of the principal ceremony was the Cathedral, which was most magnificently decorated for the occasion. The whole interior of the building was illumined with an immense number of wax candles, contained in chandeliers and branches of silver and gold, which were suspended from the arches or attached to the walls. The steps of the altar, and all that part of the pavement of the church over which the Czarina would have to walk in the performance of the ceremonies, were covered with rich tapestry embroidered with gold, and the seats on which the bishops and other ecclesiastical dignitaries were to sit were covered with crimson cloth.

The ceremony of the coronation itself was to be performed on a dais, or raised platform, which was set up in the middle of the church. This platform, with the steps leading to it, was carpeted with crimson velvet, and it was surmounted by a splendid canopy made of silk, embroidered with gold. The canopy was ornamented, too, on every side with fringes, ribbons, tufts, tassels, and gold lace, in the richest manner. Under the canopy was the double throne for the emperor and empress, and near it seats for the royal princesses, all covered with crimson velvet trimmed with gold.

When the appointed hour arrived the procession was formed at the royal palace, and moved toward the Cathedral through a dense and compact mass of spectators that every where thronged the way. Every window was filled, and the house-tops, wherever there was space for a footing, were crowded. There were troops of guards mounted on horseback and splendidly caparisoned—there were bands of music, and heralds, and great officers of state, bearing successively, on cushions ornamented with gold and jewels, the imperial mantle, the globe, the sceptre, and the crown. In this way the royal party proceeded to the Cathedral, and there, after going through a great many ceremonies, which, from the magnificence of the dresses, of the banners, and the various regal emblems that were displayed, was very gorgeous to behold, but which it would be tedious to describe, the crown was placed upon Catharine's head, the moment being signalized to all Moscow by the ringing of bells, the music of trumpets and drums, and the firing of cannon.

The ceremonies were continued through two days by several

Jacob Abbott

other imposing processions, and were closed on the night of the second day by a grand banquet held in a spacious hall which was magnificently decorated for the occasion. And while the regal party within the hall were being served with the richest viands from golden vessels, the populace without were feasted by means of oxen roasted whole in the streets, and public fountains made to run with exhaustless supplies of wine.

The coronation of Catharine as empress was not a mere empty ceremony. There were connected with it formal legal arrangements for transferring the supreme power into her hands on the death of the Czar. Nor were these arrangements made any too soon; for it was in less than a year after that time that the Czar, in the midst of great ceremonies of rejoicing, connected with the betrothal of one of his daughters, the Princess Anna Petrowna, to a foreign duke, was attacked suddenly by a very painful disease, and, after suffering great distress and anguish for many days, he at length expired. His death took place on the 28th of January, 1725.

One of his daughters, the Princess Natalia Petrowna, the third of Catharine's children, died a short time after her father, and the bodies of both parent and child were interred together at the same funeral ceremony, which was conducted with the utmost possible pomp and parade. The obsequies were so protracted that it was more than six weeks from the death of the Czar before the bodies were finally committed to the tomb; and a volume might be filled with an account of the processions, the ceremonies, the prayers, the chantings, the costumes, the plumes and trappings of horses, the sledges decked in mourning, the requiems sung, the salvos of artillery fired, and all the various other displays and doings connected with the occasion.

Thus was brought to an end the earthly personal career of Peter the Great. He well deserves his title, for he was certainly one of the greatest as well as one of the most extraordinary men that ever lived. Himself half a savage, he undertook to civilize twenty millions of people, and he pursued the work during his whole lifetime through dangers, difficulties, and discouragements which it required a surprising degree of determination and energy to surmount. He differs from other great military monarchs that have appeared from time to time in the world's history, and by their exploits have secured for themselves the title of The Great, in this, that, while they acquired their renown by conquests gained over foreign nations, which, in most cases, after the death of their conquerors, lapsed again into their original condition, leaving no permanent results behind, the triumphs which Peter achieved were the commencement of a work of internal improvement and reform which is now, after the lapse of a century and a half since he commenced it, still going on. The work is, in fact, advancing at the present day with perhaps greater and more successful progress than ever before.

Notwithstanding the stern severity of Peter's character, the terrible violence of his passions, and the sort of savage grandeur which marked all his great determinations and plans, there was a certain vein of playfulness running through his mind; and, when he was in a jocose or merry humor, no one could be more jocose and merry than he. The interest which he took in the use of tools, and in working with his own hands at various handicrafts—his notion of entering the army as a drummer, the navy as a midshipman, and rising gravely, by regular promotion in both services, through all the grades—the way in which he often amused himself, when on his travels, in going about in disguise among all sorts of people, and a thousand other circumstances which are related of him by historians, are indications of what might be called a sort of boyish spirit, which strongly marked his character, and was seen continually coming out into action during the whole course of his life.

It was only two years before his death that a striking instance of this occurred. The first vessel that was built in Russia was a small skiff, which was planned and built almost entirely by Peter's own hands. This skiff was built at Moscow, where it remained for twenty or thirty years, an object all this time, in Peter's mind, of special affection and regard. At length, when the naval power of the empire was firmly established, Peter conceived the idea of removing this skiff from Moscow to Petersburg, and consecrating it solemnly there as a sort of souvenir to be preserved forever in commemoration of the small beginnings from which all the naval greatness of the empire had sprung. The name which he had given to the skiff was The Little Grandfather, the name denoting that the little craft, frail and insignificant as it was, was the parent and progenitor of all the great frigates and ships of the line which were then at anchor in the Roads about Cronstadt and off the mouth of the Neva.

A grand ceremony was accordingly arranged for the "consecration of the Little Grandfather." The little vessel was brought in triumph from Moscow to Petersburg, where it was put on board a sort of barge or galliot to be taken to Cronstadt. All the great officers of state and all the foreign ministers were invited to be present at the consecration. The company embarked on board yachts provided for them, and went down the river following the Little Grandfather, which was borne on its galliot in the van—drums beating, trumpets sounding, and banners waving all the way.

The next day the whole fleet, which had been collected in the bay for this purpose, was arranged in the form of an amphitheatre. The Little Grandfather was let down from his galliot into the water. The emperor went on board of it. He was accompanied by the admirals and vice admirals of the fleet, who were to serve as crew. The admiral stationed himself at the helm to steer, and the vice admirals took the oars. These grand officials were not required, however, to do much hard work at rowing, for there were two shallops provided, manned by strong men, to tow the skiff. In this way the skiff rowed to and fro over the sea, and then passed along the fleet, saluted every where by the shouts of the crews upon the yards and in the rigging, and by the guns of the ships. Three thousand guns were discharged by the ships in these salvos in honor of their humble progenitor. The Little Grandfather returned the salutes of the guns with great spirit by means of three small swivels which had been placed on board.

The Empress Catharine saw the show from an elevation on the shore, where she sat with the ladies of her court in a pavilion or tent which had been erected for the purpose.

At the close of the ceremonies the skiff was deposited with great ceremony in the place which had been prepared to receive it in the Castle of Cronstadt, and there, when one more day had been spent in banquetings and rejoicings, the company left the Little Grandfather to his repose, and returned in their yachts to the town.

Not many days after the death of Peter, Catharine, in accordance with the arrangements that Peter had previously made, was proclaimed empress by a solemn act of the senate and ministers of state, and she at once entered upon the exercise of the sovereign power. She signalized her accession by a great many acts of clemency—liberating prisoners, recalling exiles, removing bodies from gibbets and wheels, and heads from poles, and delivering them to friends for burial, remitting the sentence of death pronounced upon political offenders, and otherwise mitigating and assuaging sufferings which Peter's remorseless ideas of justice and retribution had caused. Catharine did not, however, live long to exercise her beneficial power. She died suddenly about two years after her husband, and was buried with great pomp in a grand monumental tomb in one of the churches of St. Petersburg, which she had been engaged ever since his death in constructing for him.

Choose from Thousands of 1stWorldLibrary Classics By

A. M. Barnard
Ada Leverson
Adolphus William Ward
Aesop
Agatha Christie
Alexander Aaronsohn
Alexander Kielland
Alexandre Dumas
Alfred Gatty
Alfred Ollivant
Alice Duer Miller
Alice Turner Curtis
Alice Dunbar
Allen Chapman
Alleyne Ireland
Ambrose Bierce
Amelia E. Barr
Amory H. Bradford
Andrew Lang
Andrew McFarland Davis
Andy Adams
Angela Brazil
Anna Alice Chapin
Anna Sewell
Annie Besant
Annie Hamilton Donnell
Annie Payson Call
Annie Roe Carr
Annonaymous
Anton Chekhov
Archibald Lee Fletcher
Arnold Bennett
Arthur C. Benson
Arthur Conan Doyle
Arthur M. Winfield
Arthur Ransome
Arthur Schnitzler
Arthur Train
Atticus
B.H. Baden-Powell
B. M. Bower
B. C. Chatterjee
Baroness Emmuska Orczy
Baroness Orczy
Basil King
Bayard Taylor
Ben Macomber
Bertha Muzzy Bower
Bjornstjerne Bjornson

Booth Tarkington
Boyd Cable
Bram Stoker
C. Collodi
C. E. Orr
C. M. Ingleby
Carolyn Wells
Catherine Parr Traill
Charles A. Eastman
Charles Amory Beach
Charles Dickens
Charles Dudley Warner
Charles Farrar Browne
Charles Ives
Charles Kingsley
Charles Klein
Charles Hanson Towne
Charles Lathrop Pack
Charles Romyn Dake
Charles Whibley
Charles Willing Beale
Charlotte M. Braeme
Charlotte M. Yonge
Charlotte Perkins Stetson
Clair W. Hayes
Clarence Day Jr.
Clarence E. Mulford
Clemence Housman
Confucius
Coningsby Dawson
Cornelis DeWitt Wilcox
Cyril Burleigh
D. H. Lawrence
Daniel Defoe
David Garnett
Dinah Craik
Don Carlos Janes
Donald Keyhoe
Dorothy Kilner
Dougan Clark
Douglas Fairbanks
E. Nesbit
E. P. Roe
E. Phillips Oppenheim
E. S. Brooks
Earl Barnes
Edgar Rice Burroughs
Edith Van Dyne
Edith Wharton

Edward Everett Hale
Edward J. O'Biren
Edward S. Ellis
Edwin L. Arnold
Eleanor Atkins
Eleanor Hallowell Abbott
Eliot Gregory
Elizabeth Gaskell
Elizabeth McCracken
Elizabeth Von Arnim
Ellem Key
Emerson Hough
Emilie F. Carlen
Emily Bronte
Emily Dickinson
Enid Bagnold
Enilor Macartney Lane
Erasmus W. Jones
Ernie Howard Pie
Ethel May Dell
Ethel Turner
Ethel Watts Mumford
Eugene Sue
Eugenie Foa
Eugene Wood
Eustace Hale Ball
Evelyn Everett-green
Everard Cotes
F. H. Cheley
F. J. Cross
F. Marion Crawford
Fannie E. Newberry
Federick Austin Ogg
Ferdinand Ossendowski
Fergus Hume
Florence A. Kilpatrick
Fremont B. Deering
Francis Bacon
Francis Darwin
Frances Hodgson Burnett
Frances Parkinson Keyes
Frank Gee Patchin
Frank Harris
Frank Jewett Mather
Frank L. Packard
Frank V. Webster
Frederic Stewart Isham
Frederick Trevor Hill
Frederick Winslow Taylor

Friedrich Kerst
Friedrich Nietzsche
Fyodor Dostoyevsky
G.A. Henty
G.K. Chesterton
Gabrielle E. Jackson
Garrett P. Serviss
Gaston Leroux
George A. Warren
George Ade
Geroge Bernard Shaw
George Cary Eggleston
George Durston
George Ebers
George Eliot
George Gissing
George MacDonald
George Meredith
George Orwell
George Sylvester Viereck
George Tucker
George W. Cable
George Wharton James
Gertrude Atherton
Gordon Casserly
Grace E. King
Grace Gallatin
Grace Greenwood
Grant Allen
Guillermo A. Sherwell
Gulielma Zollinger
Gustav Flaubert
H. A. Cody
H. B. Irving
H.C. Bailey
H. G. Wells
H. H. Munro
H. Irving Hancock
H. R. Naylor
H. Rider Haggard
H. W. C. Davis
Haldeman Julius
Hall Caine
Hamilton Wright Mabie
Hans Christian Andersen
Harold Avery
Harold McGrath
Harriet Beecher Stowe
Harry Castlemon
Harry Coghill
Harry Houidini

Hayden Carruth
Helent Hunt Jackson
Helen Nicolay
Hendrik Conscience
Hendy David Thoreau
Henri Barbusse
Henrik Ibsen
Henry Adams
Henry Ford
Henry Frost
Henry James
Henry Jones Ford
Henry Seton Merriman
Henry W Longfellow
Herbert A. Giles
Herbert Carter
Herbert N. Casson
Herman Hesse
Hildegard G. Frey
Homer
Honore De Balzac
Horace B. Day
Horace Walpole
Horatio Alger Jr.
Howard Pyle
Howard R. Garis
Hugh Lofting
Hugh Walpole
Humphry Ward
Ian Maclaren
Inez Haynes Gillmore
Irving Bacheller
Isabel Cecilia Williams
Isabel Hornibrook
Israel Abrahams
Ivan Turgenev
J.G.Austin
J. Henri Fabre
J. M. Barrie
J. M. Walsh
J. Macdonald Oxley
J. R. Miller
J. S. Fletcher
J. S. Knowles
J. Storer Clouston
J. W. Duffield
Jack London
Jacob Abbott
James Allen
James Andrews
James Baldwin

James Branch Cabell
James DeMille
James Joyce
James Lane Allen
James Lane Allen
James Oliver Curwood
James Oppenheim
James Otis
James R. Driscoll
Jane Abbott
Jane Austen
Jane L. Stewart
Janet Aldridge
Jens Peter Jacobsen
Jerome K. Jerome
Jessie Graham Flower
John Buchan
John Burroughs
John Cournos
John F. Kennedy
John Gay
John Glasworthy
John Habberton
John Joy Bell
John Kendrick Bangs
John Milton
John Philip Sousa
John Taintor Foote
Jonas Lauritz Idemil Lie
Jonathan Swift
Joseph A. Altsheler
Joseph Carey
Joseph Conrad
Joseph E. Badger Jr
Joseph Hergesheimer
Joseph Jacobs
Jules Vernes
Julian Hawthrone
Julie A Lippmann
Justin Huntly McCarthy
Kakuzo Okakura
Karle Wilson Baker
Kate Chopin
Kenneth Grahame
Kenneth McGaffey
Kate Langley Bosher
Kate Langley Bosher
Katherine Cecil Thurston
Katherine Stokes
L. A. Abbot
L. T. Meade

L. Frank Baum	Owen Johnson	Stephen Crane
Latta Griswold	P.G. Wodehouse	Stewart Edward White
Laura Dent Crane	Paul and Mabel Thorne	Stijn Streuvels
Laura Lee Hope	Paul G. Tomlinson	Swami Abhedananda
Laurence Housman	Paul Severing	Swami Parmananda
Lawrence Beasley	Percy Brebner	T. S. Ackland
Leo Tolstoy	Percy Keese Fitzhugh	T. S. Arthur
Leonid Andreyev	Peter B. Kyne	The Princess Der Ling
Lewis Carroll	Plato	Thomas A. Janvier
Lewis Sperry Chafer	Quincy Allen	Thomas A Kempis
Lilian Bell	R. Derby Holmes	Thomas Anderton
Lloyd Osbourne	R. L. Stevenson	Thomas Bailey Aldrich
Louis Hughes	R. S. Ball	Thomas Bulfinch
Louis Joseph Vance	Rabindranath Tagore	Thomas De Quincey
Louis Tracy	Rahul Alvares	Thomas Dixon
Louisa May Alcott	Ralph Bonehill	Thomas H. Huxley
Lucy Fitch Perkins	Ralph Henry Barbour	Thomas Hardy
Lucy Maud Montgomery	Ralph Victor	Thomas More
Luther Benson	Ralph Waldo Emmerson	Thornton W. Burgess
Lydia Miller Middleton	Rene Descartes	U. S. Grant
Lyndon Orr	Ray Cummings	Upton Sinclair
M. Corvus	Rex Beach	Valentine Williams
M. H. Adams	Rex E. Beach	Various Authors
Margaret E. Sangster	Richard Harding Davis	Vaughan Kester
Margret Howth	Richard Jefferies	Victor Appleton
Margaret Vandercook	Richard Le Gallienne	Victor G. Durham
Margaret W. Hungerford	Robert Barr	Victoria Cross
Margret Penrose	Robert Frost	Virginia Woolf
Maria Edgeworth	Robert Gordon Anderson	Wadsworth Camp
Maria Thompson Daviess	Robert L. Drake	Walter Camp
Mariano Azuela	Robert Lansing	Walter Scott
Marion Polk Angellotti	Robert Lynd	Washington Irving
Mark Overton	Robert Michael Ballantyne	Wilbur Lawton
Mark Twain	Robert W. Chambers	Wilkie Collins
Mary Austin	Rosa Nouchette Carey	Willa Cather
Mary Catherine Crowley	Rudyard Kipling	Willard F. Baker
Mary Cole	Saint Augustine	William Dean Howells
Mary Hastings Bradley	Samuel B. Allison	William le Queux
Mary Roberts Rinehart	Samuel Hopkins Adams	W. Makepeace Thackeray
Mary Rowlandson	Sarah Bernhardt	William W. Walter
M. Wollstonecraft Shelley	Sarah C. Hallowell	William Shakespeare
Maud Lindsay	Selma Lagerlof	Winston Churchill
Max Beerbohm	Sherwood Anderson	Yei Theodora Ozaki
Myra Kelly	Sigmund Freud	Yogi Ramacharaka
Nathaniel Hawthrone	Standish O'Grady	Young E. Allison
Nicolo Machiavelli	Stanley Weyman	Zane Grey
O. F. Walton	Stella Benson	
Oscar Wilde	Stella M. Francis	